Paolo Maria Reynaud, M. T. ed Kelly

Another China

Notes on the Celestial Empire as Viewed by a Catholic Bishop

Paolo Maria Reynaud, M. T. ed Kelly

Another China

Notes on the Celestial Empire as Viewed by a Catholic Bishop

ISBN/EAN: 9783337170882

Printed in Europe, USA, Canada, Australia, Japan

Cover: Foto ©ninafisch / pixelio.de

More available books at **www.hansebooks.com**

ANOTHER CHINA

NOTES ON THE CELESTIAL EMPIRE

AS VIEWED BY A CATHOLIC BISHOP

BY THE
RIGHT REVEREND MONSEIGNEUR REYNAUD, C.M.
Vicar Apostolic of the District of Tché-Kiang.

With Illustrations

EDITED BY
M. T. KELLY.

DUBLIN:
BROWNE & NOLAN, Limited; M H. GILL & SON.
LONDON: BURNS & OATES, LIMITED.
NEW YORK, CINCINNATI, & CHICAGO: BENZIGER BROTHERS.
1897.

CONTENTS.

		PAGE
I.—FORE-WORD		1
II.—FALSE NOTIONS ABOUT CHINA		5
III.—A FEW FACTS AND FIGURES		11
IV.—OBSTACLES TO THE SPREAD OF THE FAITH		2
V.—PROTESTANT AND CATHOLIC MISSIONS		30
VI.—A WORD FOR THE CHINAMAN		41
VII.—CHINESE LANGUAGE AND INSTITUTIONS		49
VIII.—SOME VIRTUES OF THE CHINESE		58
IX.—THE NATIVE CATHOLIC BODY		64
X.—OUR FUTURE PROSPECTS—EVIDENCE OF THE MISSIONARIES		76
XI.—OUR WORKERS AND THEIR WANTS		88
XII.—PARTING WORDS		100

ILLUSTRATIONS.

Imperial Monument raised to the memory of the faithful widow, He-Mei	*Frontispiece*
Hospice of Aged Women at Ning-Po (Sisters of Charity)	15
The Boys' School at Ning-Po (Sisters of Charity)	25
Church of St. Paul, Wenchow	33
Brass Band of the Petit Seminaire, Chu-San	49
Native Priests of the Tché-Kiang Vicariate	65
Group of the Chu Family, Ning-Po	72
Community of the Virgins of Purgatory	92

This little work is issued by the Arch-Confraternity of St. Joseph, Protector of the Souls in Purgatory.

Any profits arising from the sale will be devoted to the education of St. Joseph's Young Priests for China.

I.
FORE-WORD.

CHINA has frequently been described in English by persons representing various interests, and therefore viewing the country through many-coloured glasses. Diplomatists and missionaries have had their word to say, as also traders and tourists, ethnologists, and strategists. Nor has the picture of the Celestials, drawn by these combined authorities, been a flattering one. Probably the prevailing impression left on the English mind is that the inhabitants of China are a villainous crew, a disgrace to humanity, as well as a menace to civilization, and good for nothing, except to be held up by superior people as an everlasting mockery.

From this view, Monseigneur Reynaud differs profoundly. He has lived with the people, to some extent as one of themselves, and it is his belief that of the China of the Catholic missionaries many good things ought to be uttered. He feels, moreover, that it would be to the no slight advantage of his cause that a larger and truer view of the prospects of Catholicity should prevail, and more especially among the English-speaking races. Having recently arrived in Europe, on his visit to the Holy See, and in order to advance the interests of the flock committed to his care, he has prepared the following notes to be published simultaneously, and with identical illustrations, in France, and in this country.

As is natural, the remarks of the Bishop chiefly refer to his own district, the Apostolic Vicariate of Tché-Kiang, which, though of recent formation as a distinct ecclesiastical territory, is not without relative importance. The episcopal residence is in the city of Ning-Po, a large seaport some hundred miles to the south of Shang-Hai, and more or less under British protection. Many Europeans are living there, and on the whole things are better from a European point of view than in places further up the country. Even the Catholics at Ning-Po are comparatively well off, especially as to the number of the Catechumens. Thus the reader will do well to bear in mind that when Monseigneur Reynaud speaks favourably of his own surroundings, we may not always apply his statements, at least in an equal degree, to the whole of China. This immense territory, we must never forget, contains eighteen vast provinces, each of which is really like a small kingdom in extent. The soil in different parts varies much, so do the

FORE-WORD.

customs, and even the religions, of the people; so that what is true of one part is not necessarily true of the rest; and the differences between North and South China are to be specially noted.

Notwithstanding the above limitations, it is almost self-evident that for gaining a clear and vivid idea of what life in China really is, a truthful and unimpassioned account of a single locality from a good authority, is worth a great deal of vague and declamatory writing from those who imagine they know all about this vast extent of country, but who have neither thrown in their lot with the people, nor even really dwelt among them. And if our authority should, upon closer acquaintance, reveal himself as something of an enthusiast for the Chinese—he would be the last to resent this accusation—yet, will it not be only too easy for the reader to find in the literature of the subject many a corrective for a too favourable impression of the 'Heathen Chinee'?

In preparing the English version, the Editor has departed but slightly from the original, and has only ventured to make to it a few trifling additions. Such as have been made consist principally of extracts from the latest English authorities on China. In many cases they appear to confirm Monseigneur Reynaud's statements remarkably, and as they are chiefly Protestant writers, they will naturally carry great weight with English and Irish readers, and possibly will add in no slight degree to their interest in the notes.

The aim of the work is a practical one. It is intended not merely to show that the gradual conversion of China is no chimerical undertaking, but also to insist on the great and pressing need that exists for priests to put their hand to the task. May it quicken zeal in many an English or an Irish heart to come to the rescue of these poor abandoned souls, either by a life's devotion, or, where that cannot be given, by help to such as will give it.

II.
FALSE NOTIONS ABOUT CHINA.

THE inquiry has frequently been made, if it can be possible to convert to Christianity a nation like the Chinese, who are supposed to be devoid of all morality, and to be endowed with the most villainous disposition. The falsity of this opinion must now be shown, and in order to do this thoroughly, it is necessary to speak of the prejudices against the Chinamen, of the local difficulties that impede missionary labour, and then to point out numerous and consoling reasons that lead us to hope for the increase and the prosperity of the Catholic missions in China.

The reputation of the Chinese, extremely bad in Europe, is particularly so in England, even among the Catholics who acquiesce in the universal opinion that in such a land as China, missionary labour is almost useless, as the natives of the Celestial Empire are incapable of conversion, and that those who are neophytes are no better than baptized pagans, possessing little faith and many vices. The missionaries are only to be pitied, wasting their time, and often shedding their blood, in such unprofitable labour. Consequently, on the strength of this widely spread delusion, it is no longer the fashion to assist the Chinese missions, and alms are bestowed elsewhere.

These false ideas about China do not proceed from the Catholic missionaries, among whom there is at present but one English-speaking priest, but rather from the traders, the diplomatists, and the Protestant ministers of Great Britain, all forming a numerous legion in China. The laity, drawing their conclusions from certain Chinese defects, as they see them, imagine that the introduction of religion is perfectly useless; while the ministers consider that if their labours be not as successful as they desire, the Catholic missionaries cannot possibly succeed either—a dangerous and utterly illogical conclusion based upon very debateable premises.

Europeans frequently speak of China without real knowledge of it, and those who write about the country say that they can confidently support their opinions as they have lived and travelled in China; whereas the truth is they all live *beside* not *among* the Chinese, at the treaty ports, which are real sinks of iniquity, attracting the wicked and corrupting the good. Those who judge of the country by these wretched specimens, are committing the error of *ab uno disce omnes*. Moreover, the intercourse between Europeans and Chinese at the ports is by no means close. Many only see the Chinamen in the streets, others draw their ideas of them from the newspapers, which criticize people who should not be confounded with the Chinese nation. The Consuls visit the Mandarins, who, under a deceitful politeness, conceal the utmost cunning, bad faith and dislike. The traders and Custom House officials are in daily contact with sharpers, expert in every kind of deception. The Consuls declare the Chinese to be a nation of liars and knaves ; and the traders add that they are all born thieves from the highest to the lowest ; an impression strengthened by the lack of good servants who are rarely obtained, while the others have to be watched as if they were enemies. The contact with western civilization seems to turn the heads of the ordinary Chinese, who imitate European defects in addition to their own vices. Nowhere are there men so absurd, more arrogant and insupportable, than certain celestials in foreign employment. The Europeans, who travel up the rivers in boats and cross the mountains in palanquins, return with the mistaken notion that they have seen the Chinese at home, have studied them well, and know them thoroughly; while in reality, not understanding the language, they have collected their information from their servants, or rather as much as these men may have chosen to give them. Seeing China in this fashion, their knowledge must be more superficial than exact, as they can only judge by the exterior, and not by the interior life of the Chinese.

"You may paint a bear," says the Chinaman, "but you can only paint his coat, not his bones; you may recognise a man's face, but you cannot know his heart." To understand people you must mix and live with them.

Moreover, there are two distinct Chinas, the official China composed of *literati* and Mandarins, and the China of private individuals. The first deserves all the reproaches heaped upon it; while the second, along with considerable defects, possesses many good qualities. It is, however, a common mistake to confound both these divisions, and to impute to the entire nation the vices and abuses of its Government. Although the Chinese code of law is remarkable for its wisdom and its equity, it is a mere collection of beautiful maxims, as all legislation is left to the sweet will of corrupt Mandarins, who make a regular traffic of justice. It should be considered that if these men do enrich themselves at the expense of the public, they are wretchedly paid, and when they visit their chiefs, or go to Pekin, they must in their turn bring a good sum to their superiors. Meanwhile the Chinese, while stoically enduring these exactions, heartily despise the Mandarins and their satellites, who are really responsible for the abuses that so forcibly strike Europeans. The Chinaman is supple and practical, and he calculates the consequences of every undertaking; he knows that violence always prevails over justice, so instead of launching boldly on the open sea, he prefers to tack along the coast, and to avoid as much as he can the Mandarins and their courts. "Cedo no rompo" is his motto.

Then there is a general inclination among the Europeans to sneer at the primitive ways of the Chinese, whom they consider an ignorant, obstinate, and stationary race, who will not advance with the times, and who presume to ridicule European customs. Infatuated with their own superiority, the Europeans are often blind to the good qualities of the Celestials, whom they offend by displaying open contempt of the natives and their habits; while, on the other hand, the sad samples of our civilization often seen at the ports, are not likely to excite in the minds of the natives respect or admiration for modern progress.

The Chinese are heathens who have not had eighteen centuries of Christianity to civilize them; but it must be admitted that with all their errors and vices, they have not fallen as low as other nations. For instance, many of the reproaches addressed by St. Paul to the Romans would not be brought by him against the inhabitants of China were he now to visit it. We may go further, and say that the corruption existing in China is less deep-seated and less visible than in certain of our western cities, the scandal of which would bring a blush to the cheek of a Chinaman who is deemed to be so wicked.

Such are the chief prejudices against China, current among Europeans, who owing to their very education and civilization, and to the prevailing mania of comparing pagans with Christians, are hardly competent to offer an unbiased opinion about the Chinese nation as it really exists.

III.
A FEW FACTS AND FIGURES.[1]

WITH its narrow and crowded streets and its 160,000 inhabitants, the City of Ning-Po, where Monseigneur Reynaud has his residence, is one of the original five treaty ports opened to the world after the erroneously styled "Opium War." It is a Chinese military stronghold, surrounded by high walls five miles in circumference, whose granite blocks are in tolerable preservation, but partially concealed by luxuriant jessamin and honeysuckle. Ning-Po, or "the city that gives peace to the waves," situated on the River Yung at its junction with another stream, is really twelve miles inland from the mouth of the river, which is protected near the sea in Chinese fashion by a smaller walled township, Chin-hai (Defence of the Sea), while a monastery on a rock in the river, and an old castle on a steep hill, are fortified by batteries to overawe the pirates who infest the seas and magnificent rivers of the Middle Empire. The City of Ning-Po is noted for its beautiful wood-carving, and for

---

[1] For this Chapter Monseigneur Reynaud is not responsible except for the statistics relating to Tché-Kiang.

gorgeous pageants occasionally held in the streets in honour of the Dragon, which is a corrupted representation of the ancient serpent-worship prevalent among the Turanian race from which the Celestials descend. There is no doubt that the Chinese do worship devils and are often possessed by them. In the terrible massacre, in 1895, of the self-sacrificing Irish Protestant missionaries, the Rev. Robert, and Mrs. Stewart, with their companions, the Vegetarians wrote on sheets stolen from their victims, " The Dragon will conquer the foreigners' God."[1] But if Catholic missionaries in

---

[1] As we shall find it a duty to pass some severe criticisms upon the Protestant missions and missionaries in China, it is pleasant to be able to pay a tribute to the beautiful life and character of an Irishman of whom his own child said, " Father never liked to be praised." However, we may mention that Mr. and Mrs. Stewart devoted themselves for nineteen years to the conversion of the Chinese in Fuh-Kien, a province larger than England, and adjoining Tché-Kiang. Mrs. Stuart, remarkable for the facility and purity with which she spoke the language, was of the greatest assistance to her husband in his work, to which both were so eagerly devoted that they offered their lives to God for the salvation of the Chinese. The same spirit of unselfishness animated their young daughter, when on that day of death she risked her life and was severely wounded, in order to save her little sister and brother; and the poor Irish nurse was killed while she tried to save the baby from the assassins. The rest knelt in prayer, while the Vegetarians plundered their rooms; and when the final moment came, one of them cried out: "Girls, never mind, we are all going home together;" and with these simple words ringing in their ears, they received their reward. The survivor of these ladies, Miss Flora Codrington, who escaped with terrible wounds, said: " She felt no pain, and she is sure the others did not ; she felt only a thrill of joy to think they would all soon be in glory together."—*Robert and Louisa Stewart,* Mary E. Watson, pp. 144, 212, 203, 216.—*The Dublin University Missionary Magazine,* October, 1895, p. 68.— (EDITOR'S NOTE

A FEW FACTS AND FIGURES.

larger numbers go to assist their brethren upon the Chinese missions, they will by their labours uproot eventually this ancient idolatry concealed under many specious forms; and they will convince numerous Chinese that their Dragon has long been conquered by the holy Mother of God, who by her co-operation with her Divine Son, in the redemption of mankind, has crushed its head (Gen chap. iii., v. 15).

The diocese of Tché-Kiang ("the crooked river") although it be the smallest of the eighteen provinces of China, contains 60,000 square miles, with a population probably over 23,000,000.[1] Before the Taiping rebellion, which was suppressed by General Gordon, this region was known to be the most densely populated in the world, until famine and epidemics diminished its number of 500 or 600 to the square mile.[2] Tché-Kiang, remarkable in many localities for its lovely mountain scenery, abounds in mulberry groves and silk worms, which form such a great industry, and the land, especially round Ning-Po, is generally fertile and well irrigated by canals, with numerous villages in every direction, frequently visited by the devoted Sisters of Charity.

Tché-Kiang was, in 1551, portion of the diocese of

---

[1] In 1886, according to Father Werner, S.J., the population comprised 8,100,000. This appears to be a misprint.—*Atlas des Missions Catholiques.*
[2] Stanford's *Compendium of Geography and Travel*, Asia, vol. i. By A. H. Keane, F.R.G.S. 1896.

Macao, the Portuguese settlement near Canton, but in the next century it was made a Vicariate Apostolic with three other districts (1659). Thirty-five years later we find Tché-Kiang a vicariate in itself, until 1790-1830, when it was joined with that of Kiang-si. In 1846, these vicariates were separated again under different bishops, and there has been no subsequent change in this division. In Tché-Kiang the missionaries are chiefly Lazarists or Vincentians, and in 1896 there were in the vicariate 10,419 Catholics, 1 bishop, 13 European and 10 native missionaries, and 5 native theological students, among a population presumed to be over 23,000,000 heathens and 5,359 Protestants. There are 35 Sisters of Charity, 29 Virgins of Purgatory, and 38 Catechists, including schoolmasters and mistresses. The Sisters of Charity in the province of Tché-Kiang have the care of a large number of hospitals, orphanages, and similar institutions. They courageously compete with the Protestant ministers, some of whom being physicians also have hospitals, and visit the sick in their homes, striving by this powerful means to push on their own work. The Sisters, comprehending the far-reaching consequences of this enterprise, carry out their visitations of the sick with the utmost zeal and success, and even influential families, including those of the Mandarins, apply to them for their remedies and care. The Sisters can go where they please, and are invited into the houses of rich and poor, where they nurse an

HOSPICE OF AGED WOMEN AT NING-PO (Sisters of Charity).

A FEW FACTS AND FIGURES. 15

immense number of pagans, and baptize every year over 3,000 dying children. Even the ferrymen will refuse taking a fee from the Sisters, so much are they loved at Ning-Po and elsewhere.

Such is a brief preliminary outline of the Catholic propaganda as it exists in a single diocese of China. From this basis, it will be possible to calculate in some way the vast work which is carried on throughout the Empire, in which there are (in China proper without including the Dependencies) 27 such districts, each with its own bishop and staff of clergy, besides four districts which are differently organized. The diocese of Tché-Kiang may be considered in a certain sense as a typical one, inasmuch as it stands midway, in numerical importance, between the very large and the comparatively small divisions. It may be useful here to give a few statistics relating to the largest Vicariate, that of Kiang-Nan (Nan-Kin), which is under the Society of Jesus. In the year 1892, it boasted no less than 96,382 Catholics, with 128 priests, 32 seminarists, and 177 nuns. There is one other Jesuit mission, that of South Pe-Tche-li, which is smaller than Kiang-nan, but is yet among the most flourishing dioceses. There are six Lazarist missions, including that of Northern Pe-Tche-li or Pekin, and the Franciscans, Dominicans, and Augustinians, are also well represented. Most of the missions are French; others hail from Belgium, Italy, and Holland.

Our readers will probably like to see some statistics

relating to the whole country. It is agreed by all the authorities that the Catholics are enormously in excess of the Protestants, but when we come to decide upon the actual numbers of the former, we find the evidence beyond a certain point difficult to deal with. It has been asserted [1] that the whole Catholic population exceeds 2,000,000. This statement, if taken to apply to the Chinese Empire, would be an exaggeration; but as a matter of fact we have been informed that it was meant to include Tonquin (which has certainly nearly a million Catholics [2]), and in this sense it is possibly true. But are there even a million Catholics at present in China? There appears to be considerable evidence that they approach, even if they do not reach, that number. In the first place we have to this effect the statement of Mr. Martin, a Protestant, who was formerly President of the College belonging to the Tsung-li-yamen, or Chinese Board for Foreign Affairs, and who is presumably well informed. We mention this evidence first, because some Protestant authorities on the subject [3] have ventured to unduly minimize the numbers of native Catholics, making out that they do not amount to more than half a million. Their desire to prove this is not to be altogether wondered at, if we

---

[1] See *Freeman's Journal*, Dublin, April 3rd, 1897.
[2] *Dublin Review*, April, 1897, p. 257. Article by E. H. Parker (who is, we believe, a Protestant).
[3] See *A Cycle of Cathay*, by W. A. P. Martin, chap. xv.

A FEW FACTS AND FIGURES. 17

consider that the Protestant missions have not, in spite of their gigantic efforts, met with very remarkable success. As to the causes of this we shall have more to say, but as to the fact we may again quote Mr. Martin, who puts the Protestant converts at fifty, or at most sixty, thousand. On this subject Miss Gordon Cumming in her charming *Wanderings in China* (1885), remarks [1] :—

"The combined converts of all the Protestant missions in this province of Tché-Kiang may number about 2,000 ; that is to say, one out of every 10,000 of the population. The proportion of Protestant Christians in the whole Empire is estimated at one in 35,000."

To return to the point we are discussing, unfortunately we have not been able to see any Catholic statistics on the subject which are quite satisfactory. The only authority we have been able to consult for the whole Chinese Empire is the *Madras Catholic Directory* for the current year, and it is evidently not very reliable. M. Groffier, in compiling his valuable *Altas des Missions Catholiques* [2] was obliged to refer to the same authority, and, besides pointing out other mistakes, he complains in a footnote that the *Directory* was so carelessly drawn up that the totals given at the foot of the various columns in several cases do not nearly correspond with

---

[1] Vol. ii., chap. xxiv., p. 52.
[2] Published, in 1886, at Strasburg. See p. 26.

the items supposed to be included in them : and we have detected in the latest edition several evident errors of numeration. Moreover, with regard to China the compilers of the *Directory* state that no returns have been received from the Vicariates : still they proceed to give statistics, without saying from what source they are drawn. Hence, we cannot attach much importance to the statement that there are at present in China proper not more than 550,000 Catholics. In Kiang-Nan there are certainly over 100,000 ; in Tsu-Chuan (according to Mr. Parker) 80,000 ; in Pe-tche-li, 3 Vicariates, including Pekin, well over 100,000 ;[1] Fou-Kien, though stated in the *Directory* to have only 34,000 Catholics, has, in reality, according to a priest who has lived in China, and who is by no means disposed to exaggerate,[2] nearly 60,000. These are, of course, the better and the more flourishing districts; but what shall we think of the statement that in Tché-Kiang there are only 7,730 Catholics,[3] whereas we have the printed returns from Monseigneur Reynaud for every individual mission in his diocese, proving the real number to be (as above stated), 10,419 ?

---

[1] In the Jesuit Vicariate of the South-East District alone, there were, in the year 1893, 40,598 Catholics. Letter from Rev. Father Becker, Superior of the Mission, in *Lettres de Jersey*, vol. xiii., p. 57

[2] The Rev. Maurice Watson, O.P., who wrote a letter in the *Tablet* in April, 1897, and has kindly supplied a few statistics for the present work.

[3] In the *Directory* for 1885, the number is stated as 12,000, which is also very incorrect.

A FEW FACTS AND FIGURES.

If we might hazard a guess[1] as to the actual truth of the question, probably we might place the number of Catholics in China proper at *three quarters* of a million.[1] If we compare this number with that of the total population of China it will appear small enough. It is, however, necessary to bear in mind that the united numbers of the Catholics of the world do not, even according to the largest computation, reach anything like the 386,000,000, which is said by the best authorities[2] to be the population of China.

If we take a different term of comparison we find the number of Catholics in China will not appear to be so insignificant. For instance, in the year 1885,[3] the Catholics of England and Wales were only about 1,300,000 (in a population of 26,000,coo). In the whole of Australia and Polynesia they were stated by the same authority to be but 672,000 : while in the whole Continent of Africa (if we exclude the Portuguese settlements of the South West Coast, which number according to a Report of the Propaganda, about a million souls), the rest do not much exceed a half million, which is *certainly* less than the total for China proper.

There is still one vital point to be considered, and

---

[1] In case a second edition of this little work is required, we hope to be able to make an authoritative statement on this subject.
[2] *Compendium of Geography and Travel*, Asia, vol. i., 1896 A. H. Keane, F.R.G.R.
[3] *Atlas des Missions Catholiques*, p. 12.

that is the rate at which Catholicity, in spite of all the drawbacks, has hitherto been spreading in the Celestial Empire. Here again we can give evidence which is consoling enough. Monseigneur Reynaud states it as his opinion that within the last fifty years the number of Catholics in China has been nearly doubled; and he anticipates that the rate of increase will be even more rapid in the future. As far as our statistics throw any light on the subject, this statement carries with it a good deal of probability. In Tché-Kiang, during the year from June, 1895, to June, 1896, the number of adult baptisms, excluding those in danger of death, is given as 406, and the number of well-disposed Catechumens as 1790. In Kiang-nan the baptisms of adults recorded for the year 1891-2 was 1,319. In North Pe-tche-li it is stated to have been about 1,000, and in Su-Tchuen several thousand. Thus it is computed that the annual number of conversions to the faith is, perhaps, rather more than 10,000. In these numbers, those who receive baptism at death, whether adults or infants, are not included; and the good work done in that way by the missionaries can hardly be computed.

This work is not intended as an exhaustive study of statistics, and we will not prosecute the subject further. We must apologise if the numbers we have been able to give are in some cases rather vague; but we think we have said enough to convince the reader of the importance of the Catholic works going on in the

A FEW FACTS AND FIGURES.

Chinese Empire. In any case the above facts and figures seem to prove that the Catholic missionaries in China, as in Hindustan, succeed far better in making some impression upon the hard surface of oriental society than do their Protestant rivals. But is this so very surprising? No, for coming eighteen centuries ago from the East, the Catholic religion must be more congenial to Orientals than the contradictory creeds of a modern religion, which is so deeply imbued with European ideas, that it is at complete variance with those of the conservative Asiatics, who in thought and in custom are much the same as their ancestors in the far-off days which were illumined by the coming of "the Light of the World."

IV.

OBSTACLES TO THE SPREAD OF THE FAITH.

IF the Chinese be not so black as they are painted, how is it that they are not yet converted in spite of all missionary efforts? It is true that China is still very far from conversion on account of its immense extent, its enormous population, and the many obstacles preventing the advance of the Gospel. The Chinese missions have passed through the fiery crucible of violent persecutions, during which the churches have been destroyed, the faithful exiled or imprisoned, charitable works annihilated, and the missionaries dispersed with their flocks in all directions. This want of priests was the finishing stroke, as it was impossible for the converts to persevere without instruction, and deprived of all religious succours, excepting in the few remote villages where the missionaries hid themselves at the risk of their lives. At present we still have too few clergy on the missions, but by reckoning the number of places occupied by Catechumens, and by a study of the figures we have given above, it is easily seen that far from being *in statu quo*, a very decided advance has been made within the last fifty years.

Independently of the obstacles raised by the effects of original sin, poverty is a great hindrance to conversion among the Chinese, who are struggling day by day to keep the wolf of hunger from the door. In many districts cultivation of opium has taken the place of the less lucrative rice-fields. Now the Christians are permitted neither to plant the poppy-seed, nor to sell the drug, and must seek some other employment, which is not easy in China where there is such competition in every trade. Though they may be convinced of the truth of our religion, these poor people hesitate to embrace a creed which may endanger their very means of existence.

Superstitious practices that enter into every detail of a Chinaman's life, from his cradle to his grave, form another great obstacle to conversion. To many Chinese these superstitions are, at most, local customs, practised merely out of human respect, while to others who are innately religious, they are of the greatest importance. Then there are the devotees, who have acquired esteem by their piety, their long pilgrimages, giving money to build pagodas, fasting for twenty, thirty, or even fifty years, during which time they have never smoked tobacco, or tasted wine, fish, or meat, and have subsisted upon vegetables, spices, and tea. These people find it very hard to renounce all their so-called merits, and to be convinced that they have been in error, and must begin their lives afresh. To these scruples is added the terrible fear of appearances—literally, "the worship of the face"—that somewhat resembles human respect in Europe, but its effects are far stronger, more general, and more tyrannical in China. To lose one's countenance among the Chinese means to become an object of ridicule, to lose caste, and in certain cases some Celestials would much prefer death to this humiliation. Now to become a Christian, a Chinese convert has to brave this dreadful ordeal, to abandon his old customs, his ancestral worship, to expose himself to general contempt, as a traitor who has forsaken the creed of "the Middle Empire" for a foreign—a European religion. But what the convert feels much more is the sacrifice he must make of ancestor-worship, which is so profoundly rooted in China, that several have considered it as the chief obstacle to the conversion of the Chinese. In theory and in practice, filial piety holds the first rank among their virtues; and there can be no greater insult, even to the lowest and most worthless Chinaman, than to call him an undutiful son. Ancestor-worship is an act of filial piety, by which children render divine honours to the memory of their deceased parents. Neglect of this duty by the Christians exposes them to the violent anger of their families and neighbours, which fact naturally does not encourage timid people to become converts. This erroneous and superstitious practice, however, makes the Catechumens adopt and cherish more readily the devotion to the

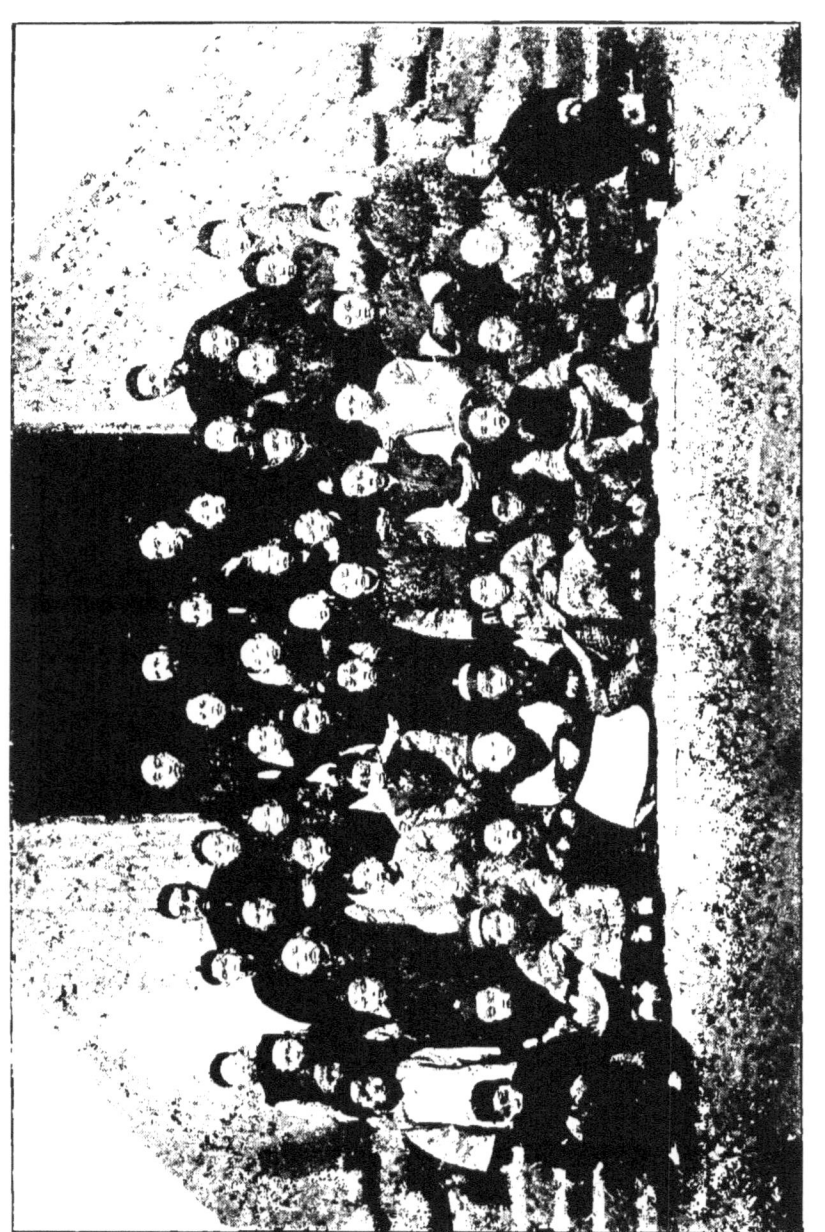

THE BOYS' SCHOOL AT NING-PO (Sisters of Charity).

OBSTACLES TO THE SPREAD OF THE FAITH.

souls in Purgatory, and this is no doubt one of the strongest attractions which they find in our faith as compared with the Protestant religion. Other manifold prejudices against our religion also deter people from approaching the missionaries.

The lies and calumnies spread by the *literati* and the Mandarins, absurd though they be, do produce some effect, and the silliest invention seems always to gain the greatest publicity and credit. Nearly everywhere the missionaries are accused of kidnapping children to use their eyes and hearts in medicines, and many are the Catechumens, who under the influence of this ridiculous notion have long deferred their conversion. Some of the Mandarins really are sincere in their suspicions of the motives that bring the missionaries to China. Being Pagans, they cannot comprehend that these priests come solely to save souls without any secret motive of self-interest. Again, the Catholic missions being under the protection of the French minister, the Mandarins imagine that the missionaries are political agents for the subversion of China. Therefore they entertain a blind hatred of the Europeans, who by their presence desecrate the sacred soil of China, and by their teaching trouble the shade of Confucius, preaching a doctrine he did not teach, and a religion he did not know—a religion, moreover, whose ethics might, by exposing their ignorance, pride, and bad faith, undermine their own power. Unable to expel the missionaries, they have recourse to the vilest accusations and falsehoods, which have been the mainsprings of the riots, which were instigated with great impartiality against both Catholic and Protestant missionaries alike. On this subject, Père Favier, of Pekin, once remarked—" In this respect, at all events, ' nous sommes tous dans le même bateau.' "

Left to themselves the people do not suspect us ; they have positively to be roused by cunning ringleaders, who excite their indignation by wicked calumnies, and urge them to such deplorable excesses. Although liberty of conscience has been imposed by the Powers upon the Chinese Government, it is not sincerely carried out by the authorities, who never protect the Christians against ill treatment. While professing the greatest civility to the missionaries, the Mandarins endeavour to persuade them to live at the Treaty-ports, where they would be much safer than among the wicked people inland, who occasion annoyance and vexations which they, the Mandarins, are unable to avert.

A Chinese mob, even a small one, excited *sub rosa* by the Mandarins is by no means pleasant company, and occasionally mission-stations are liable to sudden visitations, as in the instance about to be related. At Tai-tao-leou, in the Vicariate of Kiang-nan, on the 5th August, 1894, a band of twenty-one rioters burst into the mission-station, and seizing the Purveyor, Lieou-sin-chan, an excellent catechist, they tied him to a tree with

OBSTACLES TO THE SPREAD OF THE FAITH. 27

his own pigtail, and beat him severely, demanding money (silver ingots), and as he had none to give they wounded him terribly. Leaving him for dead, they attacked the schoolmaster and two other men, while the pupils ran to hide themselves. The whole establishment was plundered of clothing, bedding, and money belonging to the masters and scholars, and in revenge for finding so little of any value, the rioters smashed doors, windows, crockery, chapel candlesticks and statues. They also intended to torture their victims, had they not been put to flight by the sound of firearms outside the house, which, however, did not prevent one miscreant from giving a great blow to the wounded catechist, exclaiming, "Why do you follow such a religion?" which showed sufficiently by what spirit he and his villainous comrades were actuated.

China is now open to the Europeans, and the missionaries may just take their chance. The customs, the telegraphic service, and steamboats are under the direction of European laymen, all anxious to enrich themselves with Chinese money; and often leading lives which redound but little to the honour of religion. The traders only seek to inundate China with their wares, and all the foreign governments are intent on increasing each its own influence with that of China, to the detriment of the other Powers similarly engaged in this industrial conflict. The Russians on the northern frontier, the French in Tonquin, the English in Burmah, not reckoning the covetous eyes of Germans and other nations, can scarcely inspire the Chinese or their Government with any affection for Europeans, who by their disdain and contempt still further alienate the Celestials who come in contact with them. It is needless to mention the heavy indemnities the Powers impose, whenever Europeans, laymen or clerics, are injured in their persons, or have their property destroyed by the Chinese mobs. It may be objected that the Chinese should be able to distinguish the missionaries who come to China to do them good from the interested traders or Powers, who only seek their own profit. Moreover, were not the Chinese the first in the year 1893, to ask for the establishment of the Catholic hierarchy in their Empire.

To this objection it must be answered, that although the Chinese perceive clearly enough the difference between the missionaries and other Europeans, yet they confound them all in the same reprobation, and some years ago the missionaries were the people who had to suffer most from calumnies, and the incendiary fires provoked by them. As far as the Catholic hierarchy is concerned, it certainly was no feeling of affection for religion that prompted the Chinese, but simply the desire to rid themselves of the French or German protectorate. What the Chinaman really wanted, was to deprive the European powers of this pretext to extort concessions from China as indemnity for wrongs inflicted on their own European subjects or on Christians. Moreover the clauses of the concordat between China and Rome proved that no religious zeal influenced the Chinese, who were inserting conditions that would not be accepted ; such as toleration of Chinese rites, and respect for other creeds and their practices.[1]

I have now briefly indicated some of the greater difficulties we have to contend with, and we may pass on, for the present, especially as this subject will necessarily recur, being so intimately bound up with the subject we have in hand. It might have been expected that I should here lay great stress on the action of the Bonzes or native priests, in interfering with the spread o Christianity. Have they no serious propaganda to oppose to ours ? This question is soon dealt with. The Bonzes, as I know them in the Province of Tché-Kiang, ought not to inspire us with any serious apprehensions. Their bad reputation injures their influence, and their laziness interferes with their zeal. Their vocation is simply a trade, and they live by the altar, as a workman lives by his tools. Their services are indeed believed in and paid for, but their conduct wins them much contempt. I ask leave, then, simply to lay them on one side, and to pass on to the consideration of a more serious embarrassment.

Pages 58, 59, vol. xiii., *Letters de Jersey*.

V.

PROTESTANT AND CATHOLIC MISSIONS.

THE Protestants in China are very far from imitating the *dolce far niente* of the Bonzes. They are three times more numerous than the Catholic missionaries, they have plenty of means, they have also the prestige of their nationality—most of them coming from England, which is considered as a faithful and generous ally by the Chinese, who call the Protestant creed "the English religion."

It has been a question whether these three advantages of the Protestants have been injurious to the Catholic cause. Some missionaries think there is nothing to be feared, that the accusations of the Protestant ministers against Catholicity have never prevented any real conversions, and that in drawing souls away from paganism they are really opening the way for the Catholic missions. Others are of opinion that the ministers can injure their work in several ways; first by their attacks and their contradictions, which make the Chinese remark, "Since the Europeans cannot agree about religion, it is better to keep to our own." Then

PROTESTANT AND CATHOLIC MISSIONS. 31

we find that converts who have been Protestants find more difficulty in implicitly accepting Catholic dogma than those who have been heathens. Although the Catholic priests are readily distinguished from the ministers by all who are accustomed to see them, they are often confounded together by the general mass of the Chinese, and I must confess I have not been flattered to overhear them say in some new locality, " Here comes the *unquaytse* (the European devil) who sells books. Why has he not brought his wife?"

With their knowledge of the language and constant communication with Chinese of every rank, the Protestant missionaries are better able than the Consuls, the Custom officials, or the traders, to present us with a fair description of the Chinamen. Consequently they do not speak so badly of them, and some even praise the Chinese to a certain extent. Yet, notwithstanding their distribution of Bibles, their schools, the money they spend so liberally, the men they employ, and the labours in which they certainly do not spare themselves, the ministers are far from being successful. If we deduct from their proselytes, those who are attracted by wages, such as colporteurs, schoolmasters, preachers, servants, and other employés; if we take again from the number those whose faith is strengthened by pecuniary assistance, and who find they can serve their own interest by the practice of " the English religion ;" and then if we add to these the people serving two masters, who go to church on Sundays, and keep up the observance of some superstitious practice during the week, what a great reduction would be made in the already small numbers of their converts.

It is not intended in these pages to impeach the good works, much less the intentions, of anyone, but merely to state a few facts respecting the Protestant missions from a Catholic point of view; and we may perhaps be the means of rendering them some service in pointing out the weak points in their system. In the diocese of Tché-Kiang are the chief headquarters of the very numerous Protestant sects, which are to be met everywhere in China. According to their own account, there are over 60,000 converts, divided among the three branches of the Episcopal Church, nine sects of Presbyterians, six sects of Methodists, two sects of Baptists, and some others less known;[1] and all these different denominations teach their own convictions, which often clash with those of their comrades on these missions. With the exception of the Anglicans, who are usually gentlemen who have had a University career, anyone (no matter what his previous employment might have been) can become a minister, and to quote the words of Sir Henry Norman, a Protestant writer; "both men and women among Protestant missionaries are often quite unfit even to teach at home, and are not too

---

[1] *The Far East*, chap. xx., page 306. Sir Henry Norman,

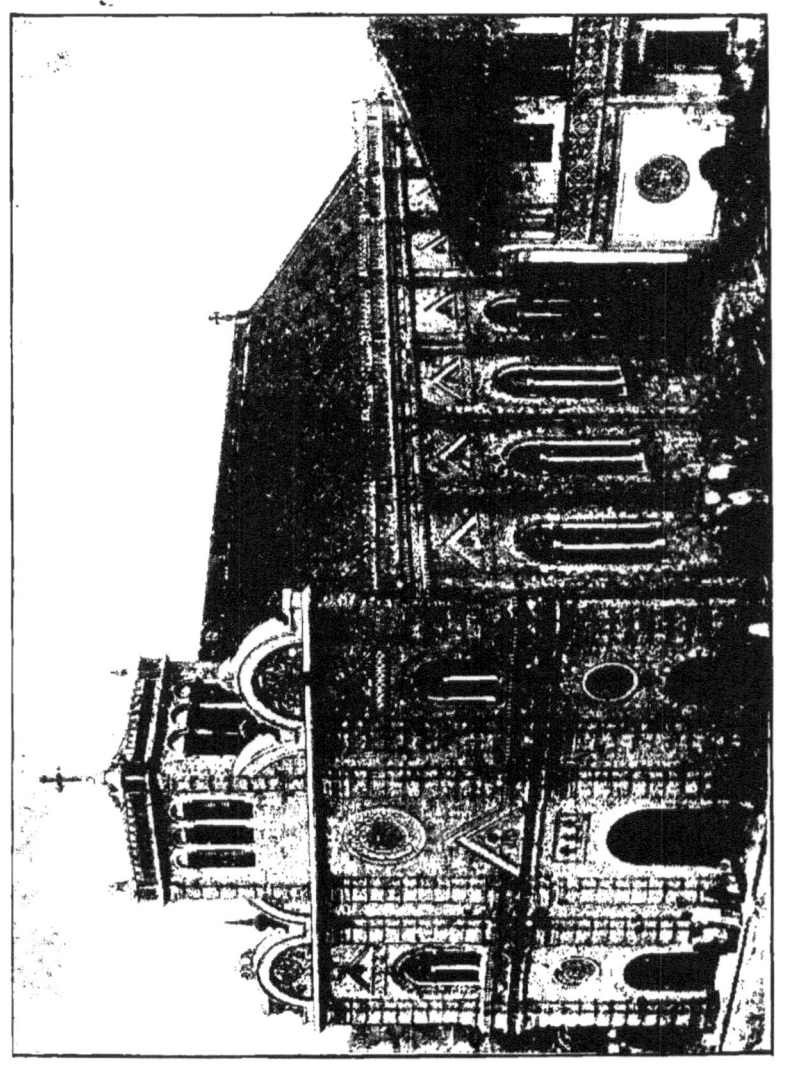

CHURCH OF ST. PAUL, WENCHOW.

PROTESTANT AND CATHOLIC MISSIONS. 33

hardly described by the phrase which has been applied to them—'Ignorant declaimers in bad Chinese.'" Sir Henry Norman, while admitting that there are among the Protestant ministers " men of the highest character and devotion, upon whose careers no criticisms can be passed," says that there can be no doubt that the Catholic missionaries "enjoy on the whole far more consideration from the natives as well as from foreigners, and the result of their work is beyond question much greater."[1]

Without then attempting to decide how far we are fettered by the presence of the Protestant missions, it is very necessary for me to give an account of their position and the progress they are making, if only for this reason. It has already been indicated that in the minds of many persons in Europe there is some tendency to confound our cause with that of the Protestants, or at least to base an opinion as to the religious position of the Chinese upon the reports which the Protestants supply.

Many of these ministers coming from England supply their want of theological science by a mystic enthusiasm which leads them into various delusions. On their arrival in China, they find no tradition to guide them, no direction to assist their inexperience. They come to replace missionaries who are going away; and in a

---

[1] *The Far East.* Sir Henry Norman.

place where all is so strange, so different from Europe, left completely to themselves, these young men, with all the good will in the world, must be liable to the most discouraging mistakes and errors of judgment. With an English newspaper we may say, if they are not to be blamed, they are at least greatly to be pitied.

The salient differences in their doctrines which are both vague and anomalous, are not lightly accepted by minds so positive, subtle, and developed as those of the Chinese, whose keen intelligence can instantly detect flaws that may long evade our attention. The incoherence of the Protestant creeds, the conflicting instructions of the ministers, are too clearly demonstrated to escape the logical Chinaman. Even the pastors lament this serious obstacle, and in their assembly at Shang-hai, 1890, they were obliged to sacrifice some of their special doctrines, and to turn their labours more in the direction of schools, hospitals, and translation of books. At present they have widened their sphere of action by a crusade against wine, tobacco, and women's small feet. To this last objection a Chinaman at Ning-Po replied in the newspaper that there were other more necessary reforms needed, chiefly as to the importation of opium, which should be first checked, and also in the custom of tight-lacing, which they declared to be more injurious to the European ladies than tying the feet is to their own. These questions may gratify philanthropists, but they will never convert the Chinese.

PROTESTANT AND CATHOLIC MISSIONS. 35

The absence of unity of belief, the rejection of authority in favour of private judgment, are radical defects of Protestantism. Now this very principle of authority is everything to a Chinese, being the foundation-stone of family and social existence, and no people have more respect for absolute authority than the Celestials. A religion that rejects this vital principle can never be regarded in a serious light by the Chinaman.

The ministers also shock the natives by their system of propaganda, which in many respects is in direct opposition to the local customs and etiquette of the country. For instance, the married pastors are more or less absorbed by the cares of family life, which naturally induces them to live as they do in Europe. They require comforts that keep them in places where they can be found, and they must have country residences in the summer, which entails interruption of divine service for that period, thereby exciting the envy of the European laity, who are unable to go to the mountains for fresh air in the hot season. The ministers must also walk out or sail in boats with their wives and children, and this appearance of husband and wife together in public is diametrically opposed to the etiquette of Chinese society.

Another obstacle is that of rendering their cause too familiar, by preaching on all occasions, inviting wayfarers into their houses to hear a sermon, offering

Bibles to everyone they meet—with the result that the most awful parodies have been made by the heathens on this sacred volume. In order to excite curiosity, some of these missionaries will offer tracts, saying, "Here is Heaven for four cash" (pence). This is rather too cheap for the Chinese, who estimate things at their money value, and who have a proverb that "Good wares are not to be sold too cheap, as cheap articles are never really good." The intention of the Protestant missionaries is good, but this exaggerated expression only lowers religion in the eyes of the Chinese. The attacks made by these sectarians upon the celibacy of the Catholic clergy do them much harm, as the heathens of this Empire hold virginity in high esteem, and cannot comprehend how men engaged in the married life can possibly be at the same time ministers of religion. Their hatred of Catholicity and their false accusations recoil upon themselves, as the pagans give us great credit for leaving all these calumnies unnoticed. By their attacks upon the Virgin Mother of God, the ministers merely disgust the Chinese, who have such an exalted idea of their own mothers that a woman has no name, but is always known as the mother of her son, "Lipa-am," "Atching-am"—the mother of Lipa or Atching. Therefore, the devotion to Our Lady is readily understood by Catechumens ; and once a whole band of pagans, on hearing abuse of the Blessed Virgin, deserted the Protestant chapel, and came to the Catholic missionary to ask for baptism.

These and other defects are the true reasons of the little success of Protestantism in China, and our cause should not be confounded with theirs, as we follow a very different road with very different results. We do not go to China to criticize manners or to destroy customs that are not at variance with Catholic doctrine, even though they be repugnant to western prejudice. The great aim set before our missionaries by Rome, the sole desire of their hearts, is to implant the knowledge of faith and charity in the souls of the Chinese. This is the polar star that directs their labours. Arriving in the country, instead of being abandoned to themselves, they find a path traced out for them which aids their inexperience. Subject to a recognised authority that prevents them from being led astray by first impressions, it is not at their own expense, at their at their own risk and peril, or by dint of groping their way through innumerable mistakes, that they learn to understand the natives and customs of their new country. From the commencement they are guided by the instruction of experienced men, and in this Chinese Empire, a perplexing labyrinth for many foreigners, they have only to follow, not to seek, the right path. Free from all ties of this world, having no family cares to distract their attention, they are at perfect liberty to follow their vocation, which is, like the Apostles, to be all things unto all men, in order to gain souls to Jesus Christ. As the Son of God came on earth to save man, so the missionaries who continue His work, set aside their prejudices and conform themselves, as far as is allowable to the manners of the people they wish to convert. This being an essential condition to ensure success, the missionaries lead the life and wear the dress of the Chinese, so that there may be as little difference, and as few causes of distrust, between them and the people as possible, and a closeness of intercourse which will enable them to smooth away many difficulties, and to study and understand the good and bad qualities of the soil they have to cultivate. At the same time by their sacred calling they are able to discern the virtues and the vices of individuals ; they come in contact with families, and in this way they acquire knowledge of many a detail connected with the life of the people. The Chinese do not consider them as travellers or mere birds of passage, but as neighbours who speak the same language, and very often as dear friends living under the same roof. In one word, China is the adopted home in which the Catholic missionaries live and die, and which they love in spite of many privations and hardships, that are not as well known as the dangers of ill-treatment and murder, and yet are the great cause of the mortality that so rapidly thins the ranks of these zealous priests.[1]

---

[1] See the remarks on this subject by Baron Von Hubner, *Ramble Round the World*, vol. ii., page 425. (Ed. 1874.)

PROTESTANT AND CATHOLIC MISSIONS. 39

Their very exceptional position, which, in some places such as Ning Po, gives them the rank of Mandarins, must give more weight to their opinions, in so far as they are based upon a more correct judgment of the Middle Empire and its natives.

We may append here the interesting remarks of Mr. Medhurst, English Consul at Shang-hai, and a Protestant, who says:[1] " It is the fashion now to complain of the Protestant missionaries, and to compare them in an unfavourable manner with their Roman colleagues ; a kind of parallel I shall avoid. The system of the Catholic missionaries is, from the first moment of their arrival, to advance as far as possible into the interior, to disguise themselves as Chinese, and to work with indefatigable ardour in the different stations occupied by the brethren for many years, if not for centuries. Their devotion is remarkable, their success astonishing ; and I am among those who think they have done, and are doing, a great deal of good. They strive to gain proselytes by means of education, a process necessarily slow, but of which the result, as regards the number and the solid nature of the conversions, is all the more satisfactory. In any town or village where there is a Catholic mission, one is sure to find a kernel of Christian families, in whom the faith has been transmitted from generation to generation ;

---

[1] *The Foreigner in Far Cathay*, published in the year 1872

and I have been often struck by the peace and look of respectability which one sees in these communities, especially when compared with the pagan inhabitants around them."

Considering the impartial and responsible character of this evidence, it would seem that its importance can hardly be overrated. It is from the Catholic missionaries that the diplomatic bodies receive the best and most reliable information as to what is going on in the most inaccessible parts of the empire, and it is evident that they are aware that no class of Europeans know China better. In the China Blue Book [1] the English Ambassador writing to Lord Granville, relating to Prince Kung's proclamation, remarks :—" We shall learn from the Roman missionaries how far this proclamation will have been spread in the interior."

•

---

[1] *Blue Book, China*, i., p. 122, published, relating to the massacres of Tien-tsin, in the year 1870

VI.
A WORD FOR THE CHINAMAN.

HAVING enumerated the vices of which the Chinese are accused, it is only fair to mention a few of their good qualities, which have been often praised by eminent Consuls, and by distinguished naval officers, who have spent much time in this country. The Chinese are intelligent, skilful, sober, hard-working, and patient. They are noted for their perseverance in every undertaking, and for the steady persistence shown on all occasions, in amassing small sums which they rightly consider as being a distinct improvement upon an empty purse. Their powers of endurance are equally remarkable in times of starvation, illness, or other privations, and it has been well said that the lower classes in China have positively reduced poverty to a science,[1] so well do they know how to turn the most trifling article of food or material to some account. Again, a Celestial will never embitter or shorten his days by "worry," that domestic fiend of the European. On account of

---

[1] *Chinese Characteristics.* Rev. Arthur Smith.

the enormous population and the immense space of ground occupied by cemeteries and tombs that can never be touched, there is no nation with more cause for anxiety as to the means of subsistence than the Chinese. So much also depends upon the absence of drought and disastrous inundations which are evils of too frequent occurrence in the Middle Empire.

Notwithstanding poverty, which is the general lot, the Chinese are to be commended for their cheerfulness, even though it may arise from the principle of fatalism implanted in Orientals. Much faith is placed in good or bad luck, which to these heathens takes the place of Providence; but no matter what they may suffer, these poor people stoically and cheerfully put into practice the saying, "What cannot be cured must be endured."

It could hardly be denied that the minds of the Chinese are very subtle, and their perceptions keen and prompt; but as they are ignorant of many subjects, they are more superficial than profound in their conclusions. However, they can be easily trained, and their aptitude for the practical side of things is a talent in itself. Even the children are more precocious than those in Europe, and they seem from a remarkably early age to develop strong bumps, as it were, of diplomatic and commercial instincts. Artistic work in China has an inimitable and original stamp of its own, which is visible in embroideries, porcelain, cloisonné, lacker, carvings, and jewellery, while at the same

A WORD FOR THE CHINAMAN.

time the Chinese will reproduce any article whatever—even to its flaws.

Expert farmers, the Chinamen use the most primitive implements, by help of which, and their ingenious fertilizers, they can raise on productive land a rotation of crops the whole year round, which are kept free from slugs, crabs, and frogs, by the ducks and fowl reared by the Chinese for this purpose, as well as for their subsequent appearance at table. The same simplicity prevails in the food, consisting chiefly of rice boiled in water, with various small dishes, to give a relish to this insipid standing dish, such as beans, peas, lentils, prepared in different ways, the best being a cheese or curd made of beans; besides these pastries, young bamboo tops, carrots cooked in vegetable oils, salted eggs, the older the better, grubs, worms, snakes, and snails are also eaten, while on the sea coast the fare is enriched by fresh or dried fish, and jelly fishes. Cows being expensive to keep, milk and butter are not used, but pork, rats, cats, dogs, and animals who have died a natural death from disease, are included in the edibles of the far from squeamish Chinese, especially on grand occasions, such as wedding feasts, &c.[1] Having a really extraordinary gift of economical cookery, a Chinaman will live where a European would starve. On the frugal fare of rice, fish, and pickled cabbage,

---

[1] *A Corner of Cathay* A. M. Fielde

the coolies will carry heavy weights, make long and fatiguing journeys, and work extremely hard (when they choose) for daily wages, amounting to five pence of our money.[1] This ability to live on little, with such small wages, enables Chinese emigrants to compete successfully with the higher rate of labour elsewhere. Many, indeed, by their thrift, actually from such small beginnings, amass enough to set up shops and godowns, by which they realize fortunes, particularly those Chinese who have naturalized themselves as British subjects at Singapore, to avoid the universal "squeeze" of the Mandarins, and the taxes of their Government at home.[2]

It should now be remarked that there is one European adage very little regarded by the Chinese, viz., that "time is money." They cannot comprehend the feverish activity and impatience of the *unquaytse* (foreign

---

[1] Economy is practised by the Chinese in every other detail of their lives. Clothes seldom varying in fashion, are intended to last as long as possible; therefore on good garments, there is scope for exquisite and artistic embroidery, which renders them heirlooms in the family.

A. M. Fielde, tells us that " the patterns and material for clothing, are nearly the same for both sexes and all ages. The shape is such, that not a scrap of the fabric is wasted in the cutting." The weight hangs upon the shoulders, and there is no compression or restriction of any muscle. While the costume is modest and protective, the amount of fabric used is small. Seven square yards or less, make a complete summer suit, and thirteen square yards, a complete winter suit, including all inner and outer garments worn by either man or woman "—*A Corner of Cathay*, ch. ii., pp. 19, 20.

[2] *The Far East*, ch. ii, p. 43.—Sir H. Norman.

devil) any more than a European admires their incredible ingenuity at deception. Calm and good-tempered, when not roused to fury or panic, the Chinese take everything as its comes ; and men as they are, and actuated by their philosophy of practical common sense, they are not disposed to be ruffled by disappointments. This apparent apathy, concealing powers of much passive resistance, renders the Chinese dangerous sophists, for possessing full control of their feelings, they are not carried away by heat of discussion, they avoid all weak points in their arguments, and discuss the most burning topics with a blandness and a subtle irony peculiar to themselves. According to the Chinese, well-bred people, if they do disagree, should explain themselves calmly and politely, while invective and threats (at which, however, the Celestials can be great adepts), are considered to indicate want of dignity and strength of mind, besides being a sure sign of defeat.

National spirit as understood by Chinamen exists chiefly among the *literati*, who have shown great inflexibility in their hostility to foreigners, although, like Shylock, they will " buy with you, sell with you, talk with you, walk with you—but will not eat with you, drink with you, nor pray with you." Among the common people no thought is given to patriotism, and this accounts a good deal for the cowardice so conspicuously displayed in the recent war with Japan, by the raw recruits from all parts of the Empire under incapable Mandarin officers. It is well known that the Chinese troops, mostly composed of coolies, mutinied, and deserted in numbers, despite the terrors of decapitation.

Speaking of the hollowness and humbug exposed during the war, Sir Henry Norman writes, that—"Against the French soldiers in Tonquin, as brave as possible, but mere handfuls in number, exhausted by the climate, badly led, and feebly supported from home, the Chinese troops won a good many victories; but against the regiments of Japan, fighting in a climate which was their own, admirably officered, perfectly armed, and enthusiastically supported, the Chinese braves have fallen back like sheep."[1] Sir H. Norman adds, however, that the Chinese seamen do not want for courage, and would fight properly under good officers whom they do not possess.

Though the Chinese certainly showed little courage during the war with Japan, still it should be admitted that had they been drilled and disciplined by another Gordon, they might have held their ground better. A Chinaman's courage can be roused by desire of plunder as among the pirates, and it can also be excited by a feud. The inhabitants of two villages at feud will fight most desperately, quite oblivious of the fact that they belong to the same race and the same

---

[1] *Far East*, chap. xviii.

country. During the celebrated Taiping rebellion, the rebels were so little deficient in valour, that their leader, a veritable Chinese "Mohamet," very nearly upset the Imperial dynasty, had not General Gordon vanquished him with the Chinese soldiers he drilled so inflexibly into discipline and unswerving obedience; qualities quite unknown to the raw levies, under equally ignorant Mandarins, who were sent to cope with the Japanese. A Chinese when goaded over much by a Mandarin's exactions will bravely attack his Yamen or Court, while he either flies in terror or tries a persuasive *pourparler* On one occasion the Celestials finding their Mandarin was taxing them far above the Government standard, came in a band to his Yamen, and destroyed all his possessions, while at the same they set a guard over the Treasury, saying that Imperial property was sacred, and should be preserved intact.

While claiming for the Chinese a certain degree of courage, which seems to be more negative than active, Monseigneur Reynaud maintains the same opinion of Chinese sailors as Sir Henry Norman. The Bishop writes that they are excellent sailors in the management of their fishing and trading junks; that he has often been on board a Chinese vessel in rough weather, and has watched the sailors, calm and determined, soothing the frightened and clamorous passengers, and manœuvring their ship with bold dexterity; while drenched by rain and deprived of sleep and food they continued their voyage across the stormy sea, without a murmur or complaint. Consequently, if they can show such qualities on board their junks, they could easily be trained on the warships were they under competent officers instead of ignorant Mandarins who do not know the A B C of naval tactics.

The knowledge of all the excellent qualities inherent in the Chinese must naturally inspire Catholic missionaries with great hope for the future of this singular people, even in spite of the strange inconsistencies of character and ideas produced by long centuries of paganism and superstition.

BRASS BAND OF THE PETIT SEMINAIRE, CHU-SAN.

VII.
CHINESE LANGUAGE AND INSTITUTIONS.

Le style c'est l'homme it is said, and it may be fairly held that the language of a people is some indication of its spirit and manner of living. The daily language of the Chinese is full of proverbial sayings, which are in constant use among them, praising virtue and condemning vice. Some of them point out the vanity of worldly honours, the contempt of riches, the avoidance of pleasures that entail so much misery, the horror of injustice, the effects of anger and impatience, the folly of pride, the iniquity of slander, the shortness of life, and so on. Others inculcate love of virtue, practice of good works, esteem of wisdom, patience in troubles, forgetfulness of injuries, fidelity, gratitude, humility, and good example. The proverbs having reference to charity are particularly expressive and beautiful; and it is to be desired that our missionaries should make great use in their sermons and instructions of these axioms in which may be heard distant echoes of passages in the Gospel. The value of these proverbs, which are accepted by the Chinese as irrefutable arguments, must not, however, be exaggerated; as there is often a very great difference between words and actions, as the Chinese admit themselves, in this local proverb, "There are people who talk like sages, and act like demons." We must not imagine that the Chinese have only these fine maxims on their lips, for many of the first sentences learned by children are full of most awful curses, and indeed some of these proverbs express very false and pagan ideas. The familiar use made by the Chinese of their proverbs seem to be a proof that they are not solely employed as a mask to deceive others, and that even those who do not observe them, acknowledge their truth, and cite them to conceal their own wrong doing. The language of an entire race cannot be one universal falsehood; and these moral notions, so often repeated, must be esteemed by individuals even if they do not always follow them; and such clear ideas of good and evil can surely be no obstacle to their conversion.

Having said so much in favour of the language of the Chinese from a moral standpoint, we may add a few words as to the difficulty which Europeans find in using it. The dialect of Ning-Po is much softer, and easier to learn than many of the others, and it also has more affinity to the Mandarin or Court dialect spoken among the officials. Yet a foreigner can easily be misled by the Chinese making the same word stand for totally opposite things, the meaning of which can only be detected by the difference of tone; for instance, in order to avert the malice or evil eye of bad spirits, great confusion purposely exists as to terms of relationship. In one family the mother will be called aunt, while a next-door neighbour will style his aunt, mother—naturally creating misunderstandings, in which exasperating propensity, the Chinese can display the most consummate ingenuity, especially where bewildered foreigners are concerned. The one word "nai-nai," mother, is used for grand-mother, great-grand-mother, aunt, and grand-aunt, and the only solution to this Chinese puzzle lies in the question, " In what degree of relationship is so-and-so to your father and mother." The following anecdote is a good instance of such a misunderstanding, although its result was exceedingly fortunate, which is not often the case on such occasions.

One day a Catechumen arrived out of breath at the mission station, and with tears in his eyes told the missionary his mother was dying. The father, thinking he meant his old Christian grandmother, fetched the Holy Oils, and hastened away. He had been twenty minutes on the road when the catechist who was accompanying him, asked "Father, why have you brought the Holy Oils, for it is not the Christian grandmother who is ill, but the Catechumen's adoptive mother, who is a pagan?" The missionary thought it was very tiresome to be taken on a long expedition to see a pagan woman, but the sudden inspiration struck him that God wished to save this poor soul, and therefore had allowed him to misunderstand the Catechumen's meaning. Accordingly the missionary hurried along the bad road praying that the Sacred Heart would grant the grace of conversion. This heathen woman had formerly adopted the Catechumen, but she knew very little about his religion, though she never opposed his conversion, and merely said that she would die in the same beliefs as her ancestors. It was dark when the missionary arrived, and at too late an hour for him to do more than send a Christian to say to the poor woman, " The father hearing you were ill, has come expressly to see you, and to exhort you to honour God and save your soul. Will you receive him to-morrow morning?" The sick woman at once asked for baptism and was overjoyed to hear that the father had come " to pour the Holy Water over her." As she was not in immediate danger she was instructed, and the next morning after Mass, the missionary questioned her, and found to his joy that she only required baptism to go straight to heaven. To prevent superstitious practices after her death, the convert sent word to all her heathen relations that she was dying a Christian, so that they should not prevent her burial according to the rites of the Catholic Church, as very often trouble arises when a pagan dies at once after baptism, and the heathens persist in declaring the baptism to be an invention of " the European devil."

We may now cast a glance upon the institutions of the country, which in a certain degree reflect its customs, and strike us more forcibly than proverbs, besides giving a more approximate view of one side of Chinese character. The institutions we speak of are societies or establishments devoted to the relief of misery, or to public works of great utility. Now the Chinese have such institutions, embracing every kind of good work, even including one for animals. Thus the English, who have a similar association, have been anticipated by the Chinamen, who have societies for the purchase of animals, and homes where they let them end their days in peace. This respect for animal life, which is traded upon by the beggars who threaten to kill serpents, as a way of extorting money unjustly, comes from the notion of transmigration of souls, in which the Chinese believe; and the dread of meeting with some unlucky ancestor or near relation under the shape of a dog, or the plumage of a cock, increases their tenderness for the lives of beasts, to say nothing of an instinctive feeling of compassion urging them to respect animals. At Shang-hai is an enormous refuge for bipeds and quadrupeds in their old age. However, there are other institutions of far greater importance than these, and the number of these is so great that only a few can be mentioned in these pages.

Orphanages.—Everybody knows of the cruelty and the infanticide which is prevalent in China. In some districts few families will consent to maintain more than one daughter, while the rest are ruthlessly destroyed as useless creatures. But it is not generally known that this barbarous custom is repugnant to many Chinese, who endeavour to extirpate it, or at least to diminish its frequency, by establishing orphanages for the reception of these innocent victims. These are to be found in all the principal towns of this province, and even in some well-known country market-places. Doctors are attached to these institutions, and the infants are confided to nurses receiving a monthly payment and some clothes. Later, the children are returned to their parents, if they choose to claim them, or else they are bought for a dollar as little daughters-in-law by poor families, or they take service with the richer classes.

Almshouses.—These are for poor old men, who are lodged and fed, and are sometimes permitted to have their wives with them in a separate apartment. Often, as in the capital of this province, each is given a small cabin, with a monthly pension of a few "cash" for food, but the pagoda, which is in the middle of the settlement, is for general use. Everyone lives and dresses here as he chooses. At the almshouse of Ning-Po and elsewhere, the food is in common, and the society provides the necessary clothing. Younger people, who are infirm or forsaken, and especially those who are blind, are also admitted into these refuges, where great liberty is allowed, of which several profit by going out begging. This is very lucrative in China, almost a society in itself, with its chiefs, its rules, privileges, and even its own little penal code. The beggars are assigned their days and stations, the limits of which are not infringed with impunity. Nearly all the chiefs are rich and influential, having their palanquins, and often living in great style, while the simple beggars realize small fortunes.

Asylums for Widows.—In China women cannot support themselves, there being few industries for them, and these bringing very insufficient wages. Poor widows, particularly those having children, who cannot or will not marry again, are exposed to starvation and very grave moral dangers; and in order to save them from these miseries, the charitable societies have these peaceful asylums for their benefit. Other widows, living with their families, are granted monthly alms, according to their necessities.

Dispensaries, &c.—There are numbers of dispensaries where patients are treated gratuitously, and druggists, where medicines can be sold to the poor at a cheaper rate, or are given for nothing. In the free schools the children are taught the classics of their country. Coffins, undertakers, and cemeteries, are provided for dead paupers, or strangers, as well as places where the dead can be kept until removed by their relations to their own district. Moreover, men are employed to keep the public cemeteries in good order. Other societies look after travellers, as well as after the lighting, cleansing and paving of streets and high roads; they repair or construct bridges and ferry boats, or build kiosques on a good site, at stated distances, where one can find fresh tea benches, and often magnificent scenery to admire.

The poor are never forgotten. At the beginning of winter, the benevolent associations distribute bowls of rice, clothes, and sometimes money. In several places hot rice can be had every day at public stoves. On New Year's Eve at Ning-Po, the leading people of the town assemble the poor in the High street, to give them clothes, rice, and two small rouleaus each in the form of "cash." Some societies undertake the care of dikes and canals, while others, in fertile seasons, collect quantities of provisions to be sold cheaply in periods of scarcity, and money even is lent without interest, to enable the very poor to gain a livelihood.

These associations, as well as others all existing in this province, have been founded by some rich families, and the Mandarins frequently issue edicts in their favour. Nearly all are sufficiently endowed, though some, such as the widows' asylums, require annual assistance, which is obtained by taxation of certain provisions or merchandize.

Though it may surprise our readers to hear of such beneficent associations among pagans, they should not leap to the conclusion that China is a land of milk and honey, where every unfortunate creature may be sure of aid; for these charitable institutions are deplorably mismanaged. Great is the robbery and waste by rapacious underlings, not to mention the utter carelessness and the various abuses to be found in these Chinese establishments, thereby forming a striking contrast to those of our missions, to the wondering admiration of the natives. Still these good works prove that there is some feeling of philanthropy among these people, and everywhere the missionaries constantly meet with souls, who, as Tertullian would say, are " naturally Christians, since they can comprehend the spirit of charity."

VIII.
SOME VIRTUES OF THE CHINESE.

BENEVOLENCE is not the only virtue known among the Chinamen. It seems to be the general belief that they are quite unacquainted with any sense of justice, and that every Celestial must be a thief from his childhood. Although equity is liable to many mischances in the midst of a heathen nation, there are numerous straightforward people, whose scrupulous honesty would excite admiration in any Christian land.

A man, originally an inhabitant of Tye-Ky, near Ning-Po, had formerly a shop for pipes at Pekin which was in a flourishing condition. He just had the happiness of having a little son, when the arrival of the rebels forced him to fly from the capital. On his return to his native village, he died, leaving his child who was too young to understand anything, quite ignorant of the past. Later on the youth heard something about the shop at Pekin, but as he knew he could never find it in such a large city, he made no inquiries. Fifty years passed, when one day an old man with a white beard was seen in the streets of Tye-Ky, with the Pekin accent. He was seeking information, but

SOME VIRTUES OF THE CHINESE.

without giving his reasons, concerning the man who had forsaken the shop at Pekin. On seeing the photograph of the man, he at once asked to see his son, to whom after very minute questions, the old man said, that he had been employed in this shop, which was confided to his care when his master left Pekin. For fifty years he continued at the trade, and now before his death he wished to give the earnings to the legitimate heir, amounting to 5,000 taëls. The heir then wished to divide the sum with the old man, or to recompense his honesty in some degree, but he refused all reward and returned to die at Pekin.

In the Sub-Prefecture of Ning-kai a peasant named Ou-te-lin had a large family, and did not even possess an acre on which to grow rice for their support. On this account he worked on hire over thirty years, and was much esteemed for his industry. As charitable as he was hardworking, he even found means to give alms. At the end of the year, when making up his little accounts he would put aside for charity any surplus over his expenses. He would not allow his wife to wash his clothes for fear she should tear them, but he would wash them himself with the greatest care, so that they might last longer and thus leave him more money for good works. Unfortunately he died a pagan, not knowing of the Catholic religion which he would certainly have embraced. However, his father, equally charitable, has now become a Catechumen.

Near the same town there is a pagan, aged eighty, justly esteemed by his neighbours as a model of probity. Although he belongs to a rich family, he has led a life of privation for sixty years, so as to be able to do more good works. Since his childhood he has only worn straw shoes, and even in his advanced age will go seven or eight miles to render a service. He has built more than forty bridges over the mountain torrents, and paved miles of roads. His last work is a bridge of three arches over a swift river, where every year many were drowned trying to ford it, and to defray the expense he sold part of his property, keeping, with the approval of his family, just enough for their maintenance. Can it then be said that men capable of such charity can never become sincere Christians?

There is also another virtue, which more than charity or justice, is supposed by some to have no existence in China, and that is the virtue of purity, which is neither unknown nor despised by the Chinese, especially in the country places where they are naturally simple, just, and virtuous.

The assertion that there has been more than one Chinese Lucrece may be disputed; but although it may be easier to discover, than to speak of, those who have by a voluntary death expiated an involuntary outrage, still the difficulty may be avoided by recounting two cases, in which there are no repugnant features.

I have frequently seen triumphal arches or monuments

in sculptured stone erected to the memory of people remarkable for their virtues, and among these were many commemorating the continence and fidelity of widows, in refusing advantageous marriages. One of these arches has been recently erected by order of the Emperor in memory of Kiou-He-Mei, a girl who was betrothed to a neighbour, who died a few years later. Her parents being already dead, her nearest relations insisted that she should be betrothed again. She so steadfastly refused her consent that her relations, without her knowledge, secretly signed an engagement of marriage on her behalf. The wedding day approaching, it became necessary to prepare her wedding clothes, and to inform her of what had been done. Kiou-He-Mei indignantly replied that they had deceived her shamefully, and that she would die, as she had lived—a virgin. As nothing could shake her determination, her discomfited relatives spread the report that the bridegroom's family would not accept their niece. These people, on the contrary, being most anxious for the alliance, on account of the bride's excellent character, brought the case before the Mandarin, begging of him to force He-Mei to fulfil the contract. The Mandarin, influenced by his wife, took pity on the poor creature, and avoided any decision by departing on a journey. During his absence, the bridegroom's family bribed one of the chief assessors of the Mandarin's court, who vainly tried by violence and threats to compel He-Mei to give her consent. In despair, and not knowing how to escape her fate, she hanged herself in the court where she was imprisoned. On his return, the Mandarin forced the assessor to bury her with the same honours he should pay to his own mother, and he further petitioned the Emperor's leave to erect a monument that should remind everyone of the tried virtue and courage of the unhappy Kiou-He-Mei.[1] Many young people having heard her sad history have refused to leave the paternal roof.

A-Kane, a young pagan girl at Ning-Po, had always an aversion to marriage. Having come to learn embroidery from the Sisters of Charity, she also acquired a great devotion to our Blessed Lady. Her mother, desirous to marry her against her will, recalled her home, where she still lives, longing for baptism, persevering in her resolution to remain single, praying to the Blessed Virgin, and avoiding work on Sundays. However, she knows that soon she will be shut up in a palanquin, and sent to the bridegroom's house. When that day comes, she will not commit suicide, which she is aware is a great crime; but she will cut off all her hair, and hopes on this account she may be returned to her parents.

The Chinese have the utmost respect for the proprieties of social intercourse, in which great reserve is maintained between men and women. It is really

---

[1] See Frontispiece

surprising to see such strictness and decorum and absence of familiarity in the manners of a heathen nation. The women are remarkably modest in all their actions; they rarely speak to the men, and are satisfied with the society of people of their own sex, even when there are family gatherings, and as it has already been observed, the Chinese are scandalized by the very different manners of the Europeans, which, in their eyes, appear to be exceedingly frivolous and indecorous.

IX.
THE NATIVE CATHOLIC BODY.

OUR aim hitherto has been to show that, even taking the pagans of China as they are, they are not so utterly depraved as to leave us no hope of their conversion. It has been our deliberate aim to dwell on those aspects of Chinese life and character, which show them at their best, in order to undermine, as far as possible, the belief that they are so bad that it is better to leave them alone; in other words, that they are "beyond redemption."

We may now leave the region of mere probabilities, however interesting they may be, and turn to a different sort of argument; we may consider the standing and the conduct of those of them who have actually renounced paganism, and have fallen under the influence of the Catholic religion. We may now consider whether the waters of baptism have not purified their hearts, enlightened their minds, and changed their mode of living? As we must estimate our hopes of the future by the results of the past, this question is important, bearing as it does on the arguments for and against the conver-

NATIVE PRIESTS OF THE TCHÉ-KIANG VICARIATE.

THE NATIVE CATHOLIC BODY. 65

sion of the Chinese. It is really a fact that we have excellent Christians among them, loving religion, and understanding its obligations, which they regularly fulfil in spite of obstacles and often painful sacrifices.

Of course we may have careless or even vicious people, but sooner or later they turn over a new leaf; while apostacy is a rare occurrence, as everything is done to test the reality of each conversion, and no pains are spared for the instruction of Catechumens. In a land like China, where abuse of authority, bad administration, love of litigation, and a vengeful spirit are rife, if we were to open our doors to everybody, we should quickly be overwhelmed, and our whole time absorbed in settling the quarrels of the people. Moreover, there is the danger of unwittingly posing as champions of unjust causes, besides the risk of opposition to the Mandarins, who, at best, barely tolerate us. Religion also would suffer, as the converts would be accused of interested motives in joining us. Hence it is very necessary to be most particular in the admission of Catechumens, and to reject all who come to us with lawsuits. Before pagans can be inscribed as Catechumens, they must renounce all superstitions, destroy their idols, begin to learn the catechism and their prayers, and to live as if they were already Christians. When possible, they also have a period of probation in our settlements, where they are imbued with the spirit of Christianity, and by good example are trained in the maxims of the Gospel. The missionaries constantly catechize them, and explain every difficulty. In their own homes, too, they devote themselves to the study of Christian doctrine, and they often sing their prayers during their work, or repeat lessons while travelling, and some will even pay heathens to teach them to read quicker. Many of these people are illiterate ; others are advanced in years, and the greater number are occupied supporting their families, so that it requires courage to undertake the learning of prayers and the catechism. The women are even worse off, as they generally cannot read one word. On an average the instruction and testing of Catechumens lasts a year, and after baptism, they are subjected to a rule that prevents their forgetting what they have learned. Every Sunday the Christians assembled in the Church must recite aloud the catechism, so that it is gone through several times in the year. At the annual confession, the missionaries ask each one questions from the catechism, which obliges the people to recollect what they have been taught. Experience has proved the value of this rule, which is rigorously enforced in this province, and in many other vicariates. Our Christians thus carefully instructed are usually pious and fervent, having an instinctive horror of the superstitions around them, and we have occasionally to moderate the zeal of those who are too ready to express their contempt. At the same time it should be observed that some of our neophytes are really confessors for the faith, owing to the tortures

THE NATIVE CATHOLIC BODY. 67

and ill-treatment inflicted to enforce compliance with local superstitions. Their fidelity is more to be lauded, as very often they are given the option of a small fine, which they steadfastly refuse to pay. Our Christians are most attentive to their devotions, and family prayer is a general rule. They are very fond of the Rosary, the fifteen mysteries being sung at intervals in the Church on Sundays. Many old people spend their whole time praying, and there is great devotion to the Blessed Sacrament.

One day a Christian woman at Ning-Po came at six o'clock in the evening to ask for Holy Communion. The astonished missionary replied it was impossible as she should be fasting, and that she would do better to look over her catechism, which she seemed to have forgotten. "Father," said the woman, "I know my catechism, and I am still fasting notwithstanding this late hour. But I have a brutal husband who prevents me coming here; and as he went on a short journey to-day, I profited by his absence to prepare for Holy Communion. Pray let us hasten, as should he return before I do, I shall be beaten." The missionary accordingly heard her confession and gave her Holy Communion.

Communions are frequent, and the young men go once a month to confession. Lent is so strictly observed among them that it has not been thought expedient to publish the mitigations allowed elsewhere.

The Catholic Chinese have great faith in the intercession of Our Lady. In one village, where a single room used as a chapel, could not contain the 200 Catechumens, matters were rendered still worse by the river (after the fashion of Chinese rivers) threatening to leave its bed in order to flow in the direction of the poor chapel. A vow was made that a good church, dedicated to the Queen of Angels, should be erected if by her intercession this misfortune could be averted, and on Sundays the Christians were to chant the Rosary for this intention. A few months later a small island formed in front of the chapel, and the river retreated more than a mile away from its dangerous course, while actually rushes and reeds have grown upon this immense extent of ground abandoned by the river Kiang. A dike was to be made as well as irrigating canals, and soon, as if by magic, fine harvests were expected to spring from the new and fertile soil. In consequence of this successful appeal to Our Lady's intercession, many pagans have become neophytes, and the Church of Our Lady of the Angels now has plenty of room for its congregation.

We have just lost an old patriarch in the village of Ma-pong, who used to spend long hours adoring the Blessed Sacrament, and on his return home he would read the *Lives of the Saints*. He was not the only one to visit the Church, where fervent Christian women come to kneel in turn before the tabernacle, and on Fridays they assemble for the devotion of the Way of the Cross The Little Office of the Blessed Virgin is a favourite devotion among young girls. Those who are unmarried recite it every day together, when there are several in the same village. Their example is sometimes followed by married people; and one day on entering the chapel of Chan-lin to read his breviary, Monsigneur Reynaud was greatly surprised to find there a man and woman reciting their office aloud, answering each other like two choirs. They were the catechist and his wife, who were in the habit of doing so every day. The Chinese kneel in the Church the whole time during their prayers, which they also sing aloud. So melodious and devotional is this chant that one could spend entire days listening to it, and it is the general opinion of European and Chinese missionaries that even the saints in heaven could not sing more divinely.[1]

Speaking of the virtues of the Christian life, the practice of them is well known to our neophytes. They have the faith, the true faith, a lively faith. As I write

---

[1] However, on the principle that every eye forms its own idea beauty, it may be remarked that there can be a difference of opinion concerning the musical abilities of Chinese Catechumens so highly extolled by Monsigneur Reynaud. An English lady, who is a member of his flock, described the first Sunday in China as " one long attempt to suppress mirth at the fearful uproar going on during Mass and Benediction, when every Celestial in the congregation sang in his own favourite key. He who squalled loudest, prayed best, while some fervent women kept up a high soprano in a nasal organ. All the devotions are sung in the same fashion, and the Chinese appear able to go on like wound-up machines." But there is no accounting for tastes.—(EDITOR'S NOTE.)

my mind reverts to a young catechist, who knows his religion almost as well as an aged theologian, and perhaps practises it better. He might be well ordained a priest at once, only that he happens to be married. But I have no loss on that account, for his eldest son is in the seminary, and he is even more like his father in his moral, than in his physical, qualities. When there is question of gaining souls for this good man, nothing can stop him, nothing can fatigue him, neither distance, nor hunger, nor bad weather. His life consists in doing good, and in preaching, expending all his strength and his money. How often has his mother come to me, with tears in her eyes, begging me to moderate his zeal. "He will kill himself," she says, "he forgets to eat and to sleep, he has no time except for the service of God and his neighbour." Affable and modest as an angel, no one can resist him. It is a pleasure to hear him exhort the dying and preach to the pagans; and it is even more beautiful to see him practise humility, patience, and all the Christian virtues. His heart seems to be set on things above this world, for which he has a true contempt.

A few pages back, I was speaking of another edifying Christian, whom we have recently lost; it is now time to mention his sister. Possessing superior qualities, handsome, intelligent, kind-hearted, and endowed with good manners, she has devoted them all to God, and for thirty years has been at the head of an orphanage which

THE NATIVE CATHOLIC BODY. 71

she manages admirably. Far from receiving a salary, she spends her own means on this institution, and she would like to leave to others the care of the big strong orphans, so that she might have to herself all the small weakly children including idiots and other invalids. Incapable of doing anything wrong, this innocent soul imagines she does not love God enough, her humility being as profound as her charity; while her patience and her tenderness gains her the love of all the orphans. Her nephew Koang-yao resembles his aunt in all the Christian virtues. As a distinguished scholar he had more chance of obtaining his degree than his comrades; but he preferred a simple life to the false glitter of worldly honour. As a physician renowned among the Chinese, he also prefers attending the poor gratuitously, to the rich who would pay him well. He helps his aunt in the care of the orphans, and is the purveyor of the establishment in spite of the trouble it entails. His spare moments are spent in reading religious works with which he is so well acquainted, that he is quite a theologian. One of his sons is a Seminarist, his eldest daughter according to a family tradition has entered a community, while her only sister lived unmarried with her parents, and never went out anywhere except to the chapel and the orphanage. With talent like her aunt she strove to imitate her piety, virtue, and recollection. At the age of twenty-seven she died like a little saint which was the name given her in the village. Her third brother threatens to follow her soon, his already broken health having been greatly shaken by the loss of his wife and child. Though quite resigned, he is preparing for death, which he neither fears nor regrets, by giving his means to charitable works. There are many other families like this one; for instance, the family of Chu, at Ning-Po, every generation of which gives a priest to the Church, and at present the eldest daughter is a Sister of Charity, the second a postulant, and the third a Virgin of Purgatory. This family has been photographed in a single group, which is reproduced on the opposite page.

Speaking of native religious, I may remark that there is a community of nuns composed of women from the best Chinese families, devoted to prayer and good works for the souls of Purgatory; and there are also excellent Chinese Sisters of Charity, whose yellowish complexions under the cornette alone distinguish them from their European sisters. They will be of the utmost use by going out wherever they are wanted in bands, to work as school-mistresses and catechists, to instruct girls and women. This is of the highest importance, as it is contrary to Chinese etiquette for the missionaries to approach them, and it is most essential that the mother of a family should be the first converted, for she will bring after her the husband and children, and keep them to the practice of their religion. So convinced are many missionaries of this, that they often refuse to

GROUP OF THE CHU FAMILY, NING-PO.

THE NATIVE CATHOLIC BODY. 73

baptize the men without their wives. The Catechumens being now so numerous, it is impossible for them all to journey down to the large mission stations as they used to do formerly, and whole villages are apparently waiting until the women can be instructed.

The following remarks will show the importance of Chinese nuns, on the mission where there are 100,000,000 women ignorant of the Christian religion :—" The state of degradation to which heathenism has brought the women and girls of China is truly pitiable. The higher classes are secluded in their own homes, just as in India, and spend miserable aimless lives, almost their only occupation being smoking, drinking tea, and embroidering tiny shoes for their poor crippled feet. You rarely find one among them who can read, or is in any way educated.

But though we speak of the ignorance and degradation of the women of China, they are by no means naturally stupid. On the contrary, where they have opportunities given them for developing their mental powers, they show themselves to be an intelligent race, well repaying the trouble spent in their teaching and training."[1]

There are also native missionaries, Chinese priests who say Mass, and fulfil every sacerdotal duty, and they are invaluable by their tact in managing business,

---

[1] Written by the late Mrs. Stewart, *Dublin University Missionary Magazine*, p. 23, October, 1895. This is Protestant evidence ; but none the less valuable on that account.

and by introducing the Catholic religion into regions where otherwise it would be rejected as a foreign institution. Their respect for authority, their zeal for conversions, and their unaffected piety render them worthy of our gratitude and esteem.

It may then be asked if there be such good Chinese priests, where is the urgent need of more European missionaries? But the answer to the question is simple enough. Though the native clergy are of such assistance, they are unable to have the sole charge of districts as large as great European dioceses, without the guidance of a European missionary. Many cases arise in which, by his superior knowledge and experience, the latter is better able to give a decision than his Chinese comrade, who is not so capable of directing other people. The general rule, therefore, is to place a European priest at the head of a mission, with one or two native missionaries as his curates. Even at Pekin, where there are old Christian families of three hundred years' standing, the Chinese priests require the support of a European missionary. How much more do they require him in the Vicariate of Tché-Kiang, where the Catechumens are nearly all new Christians. The missionaries are of opinion that it is only after four generations that the Chinese can be thoroughly imbued with the spirit of the Catholic faith. For this reason, only Chinamen whose families have been Catholics for two or three centuries, are admitted to the priesthood

Converts of a recent date are never accepted without a special dispensation, which is seldom applied for, and which is still more seldom granted.

Baron Von Hübner, in his book of travels, says that the native priests "eagerly seek theological discussions, but, more subtle than profound, they rarely go beyond a certain point in science. Vis-a-vis European missionaries they feel, and sometimes resent, their inferiority, but if treated with gentleness and discernment they become excellent fellow-labourers. With regard to morals, they leave nothing to be desired. They have never yet been promoted to the higher grades of the hierarchy."[1]

---

[1] *Ramble Round the World*, vol. ii., p. 423.

X.
OUR FUTURE PROSPECTS.—EVIDENCE OF THE MISSIONARIES.

WHAT we have said about the native Catholics of China, people and priests, may lead the reader already to surmise that, numerous and grave as are the obstacles to the complete success of our Chinese mission, they may not prove to be insurmountable. The Chinese have a proverb which says, "True gold does not dread fire." Now we have shown that the Chinese converts have stood this test in the past, and that they are standing it now: hence we may conclude with the proverb that there is some "true gold" among them. And really when we consider their sincerity as I have described it, when we consider that at the call of grace they have trampled under foot all human respect, and have voluntarily exposed, and do expose, themselves to insult and persecution, how can we imagine China to be a country invincibly opposed to the progress of religion and the ethics of the Gospel? On the contrary, the alms of the faithful and the labours of the missionaries have not fallen upon an arid soil, nor has the word of

OUR FUTURE PROSPECTS.

the Gospel been like a seed lost, or stifled among thorns; but, as will be seen still further by the results to be recounted in this chapter, it is striking very deep roots indeed.

Most of the obstacles to the conversion of the Chinese do not arise so much from the faults of individuals, as as from the hatred of the Mandarins, the calumnies of the *literati*, and family persecution ; and as it has already been observed, it is chiefly the absence of real liberty, and some want of courage, that we have to take into account in reckoning the chances of Catholicity in the Celestial Empire. At the risk of some repetition, we may say here another word on the qualities of the Chinaman that are supposed effectually to bar all chance of his conversion. But even granting the worst— granting that the Chinese are addicted to cupidity, pride, lying, cheating, and thieving—all of which vices are especially opposed to our religion, which breathes charity, justice, humility, purity, devotion, and truth : certainly the above dispositions are not of themselves a proof that the earth of the Chinese heart is in a favourable condition for being tilled. But instead of the above enumeration of vices (which it would be easy to prolong still further), why not say in one word that the Chinese are still pagans, and in this respect are the same as other pagans ? If the above-mentioned catalogue of vices was the peculiar and exclusive heritage of the Chinese, and a sort of infallible mark by which they might be distinguished from the rest of mankind, pagan and Christian, how many Chinese, alas! would be found outside of China, and even in civilized countries! The invasion of the Yellow Race which so many thinkers fear for the future of Europe, might be thought to have commenced already—perhaps to be far advanced.

On the other hand, if the Chinese were altogether free from the vices which are, with more or less justice, imputed to them, they would then be our superiors, and would be no longer in need of conversion. We should go to them for the purpose of imitating, and not of converting, them : if conversion means not merely passing from one altar to another, but also includes a complete change of life along with a change in one's beliefs. If then the Chinese are bad, they are all the more in need of our compassion and help, especially if, as I have tried to show, in spite of their vices, which are common to all heathens, they have also several excellent qualities that can only facilitate and consolidate the work of their salvation.

One defect which I have referred to above, the superstitious character of the Chinese, must now again come for a moment under consideration. We have seen that in certain respects their superstitions may be considered as a serious difficulty in our way. Here, however, I should like to point out, what I have not hitherto remarked, namely, that even their erroneous beliefs may in a certain sense count in their favour, inasmuch as they may sometimes tend to show a strong yearning after the Supernatural. After all, an indifferent pagan, having no faith in his idols, no idea of a future life, or regarding it as the veriest fable, is prone to be far less susceptible than the others to the arguments of the Catholic priest. I may as well give an instance here of the conversion of a very superstitious person. A hump-backed man on the island of King-Tang has four grown sons who are already grandfathers. The very numerous family were all converted, excepting the wife of the second son, who resisted all efforts for her conversion to a religion the very name of which was enough to put her in a fury. She did all in her power to dissuade her husband, who on the day of his baptism could find neither socks nor shoes, and had to appear at church barefooted, which looked very odd in contrast with his fine clothes, which his wife forgot to hide as well. Conquered by her husband, at least she refused to allow her children to be baptized, and when the missionary paid a visit, she would go to the female bonzes to pray with them; or else she would remain to make a noise, scolding her children, laughing with the neighbours, or rattling cups and saucers during Mass or sermon, and by way of protest she was most fervent in observance of local superstitions and idolatrous practices. One day her husband, very seriously ill, said to her: "I am dying because you will not become a Christian." She replied: "I will become a Christian only if you are cured." This was requiring a miracle, as the man's life was despaired of; however, he had a dream,[1] and on awaking told his wife to go to a certain mountain for a particular herb which she would find there, adding the Blessed Virgin had just told him this herb would cure him. The wife obeyed his order, and the infusion prepared from this plant cured him immediately. Overjoyed, the wife kept her promise and prepared for baptism, and the first time she saw the missionary, she fell on her knees and begged he would baptize her children as soon as possible. Now, whenever he comes, she prepares the tea and refreshments, prevents all noise during Mass, and takes care to call everyone to prayers, and by her fervour and good example she endeavours to atone for her former behaviour.

Although we have met with those who were perfectly insensible to every religious feeling, yet in the province of Tché-Kiang (which is one of the most superstitious in China), the greater number of the people do believe in something. Above all, they believe that it is not in vain for people to live well in this world, as in the next there is a heaven and a hell, representations of which

---

[1] The Chinese Catholics have often great confidence in dreams, and perhaps their faith is rewarded. At least Monseigneur Reynaud appears to quote this instance as though the dream was probably in a certain sense supernatural. He does not advert further to the question, but our attention has been drawn to it from another source.—(EDITOR'S NOTE.)

OUR FUTURE PROSPECTS.

in the pagodas are often shown by their bonzes, and they have an expressive proverb, saying : "The good will have the recompense due to virtue, and the wicked the chastisement due to evil ; and if this retribution has not yet come, it is because the time for it has not yet arrived."

The anxiety of the Chinese for a happy eternity prompts many of them to make painful vows, to undertake distant pilgrimages or long and rigorous fasts, which often last a lifetime. I know of one poor widow who for twenty years had been saving for a pilgrimage, and at last sold her cow, which was her most valued possession, in order to fulfil her vow before death.

The bonzes, who kneel motionless before their idols, while one by one their fingers are consumed by a piece of burning incense ; the rough hermits, who fly from the world to shut themselves up in cold grottos among desolate mountains, where their severe penances involuntarily recall to us the lives of the Fathers in the desert ; what motive but the thought of a future recompense could reconcile them to such cruel mutilation, such frightful privations?

The spirit inspiring such practices may often be less an obstacle to conversion than a remote preparation, proving that there is plenty of good will, although it is for the time unfortunately turned in the wrong direction. As a rule, the heathens do not offer any serious defence of their false beliefs, nor do they try to oppose our doctrines. Once their naturally subtle minds are open to conviction, they comprehend quickly enough that their superstitions are as ill-founded as our dogmas are worthy of the highest respect and veneration. If they have followed a false religion, it has been through ignorance of the true faith, and because they could find nothing better in their own country. Therefore, we may assume that as far as the conversion of the Chinese is concerned, their very proclivity to superstition may be turned to good account.

Leaving once more considerations of a theoretical nature, I will proceed to deal with an assertion sometimes made, namely, that conversions *en masse* are no longer possible in China. Now the falsity of this statement can be best contradicted by events that occur in this very province, where on all sides we are invited into large villages, and deputations are sometimes sent to us by entire cantons. Overwhelmed by these petitions, my own missionaries no longer suffice for the work, and on all sides they are begging for helpers. The best proof I can give for this is to lay before the reader a few extracts from their letters, which will give some idea of their labours and of their hopes.

Monsieur Louat writes : " The town of Lo-tsching continues to afford us much satisfaction ; Catechumens abound everywhere, and we have merchants and even *literati* among them. With a chapel and a missionary here, there would soon be a flourishing congregation.

OUR FUTURE PROSPECTS.

I have just visited the two Sub-Prefectures of Pin-yan, and Che-ngan, where conversions are rapidly extending, and if we had more help the progress would be much greater. The innumerable converts at Sien-tso had not been warned of my arrival, but they came in crowds last Sunday from a distance of three to four miles. The Church cannot hold them all, and half the congregation heard Mass outside. A deputation from Kin-Shiang in the South of Pin-yan, came to beg of me to go back with them to preach to many converts who had never seen a missionary, but believed heartily in our religion which they heard of from other Catechumens. Much to my regret I was obliged to defer this journey on account of all my work at Pin-yan and Che-ngan. In the last-mentioned place, the majority of the inhabitants think it would be well to have us, while some announce their determination to oppose our coming there. We are offered houses everywhere, and we shall be well received, as even *literati* have joined in the general wish for our arrival. The town is the first in my district, but, as at Pin-yan, one missionary cannot do all the work, a chapel and a school are required, but, aware of your poverty, I do not indulge in these dreams, which could easily become realities had we the means. Passing by Hong-Kiao I found our Christians very quiet. It is the largest market-place in the Prefecture, and on certain days attracts thousands of peasants. Our little congregation has increased so fast, that at every visit

I have to employ one whole day in making the acquaintance of our new recruits. If we could only be established there; if we were not so poor, and so few; if so many souls were not thereby the losers, I should not complain."

This letter gives only a passing glimpse of three or four stations, and there are twenty-seven in that district, all expanding. Among these should be cited the immense Prefecture of Tsu-tcheou-fou, with ten Sub-Prefectures, and thousands of inhabitants. This is a poor and mountainous district full of upright men belonging to various religious sects, who seem ready to embrace the true faith. A very curious caste of people live beside them, differing completely in manners, language, and dress. These are the A-Kha, or exiles and emigrants from other places. They lead their own life, do not intermarry with the natives, and live in cabins made of straw at the foot of the mountains. They are a finer and more robust type of men, and their honesty is so remarkable that they would make splendid converts. I should like to have a dozen missionaries there, and we have only one catechist.

Ouen-tcheau is the most ill-conditioned Prefecture in the province, being the abode of pirates, and a population so dense that it cannot be supported on the land fertile as it is; therefore, many are driven to live at the expense of others. The Mandarins and the rich tremble before the pirates, some of whom by their bravery are almost heroes fit for a novel, and one man was so powerful that to weaken his influence the authorities made him a Mandarin! Strange to say this region is also the most pious in the province, having as many bonzes as pirates ; and there is a sarcastic saying that if there be two boys in a family, the elder becomes a pirate, while the younger is to be a bonze, that his continual prayers may expiate his elder brother's misdeeds, and avert the anger of heaven from the family. The monasteries are to be found everywhere, and the bonzes in this district enjoy a better reputation than elsewhere, although superstition is rife there. Their influence is so enormous that if we convert one of these men, his example is certain to be followed by entire villages.

Here is one of the last letters received from Monsieur Lepens, who is in charge of this district:—" More than a thousand Catechumens from Po-yen came to San-Kiao for the feast of the Assumption. They have eaten thirteen bags of rice, for which they paid as well as for their other meals here. At Po-yen the conversions are *en masse*, and what is to be done ? There should be a missionary station at Hai-men, as the river is inconveniently in the way on account of the tides and the insufficiency of boats, so that the people starting at midnight do not reach the church till the next evening Five or ten chapels in central situations are needed, but where are the funds ? Should not an effort be made for the salvation of so many thousands? A Chinese priest has visited Sien-kin, where the Catechumens despaired of ever seeing a missionary. A Protestant European came to argue with him, and his thirty followers threatened to fall upon us if we came there; and the priest had much trouble quieting our Catechumens, who they say number 10,000. Two cantons have joined as under the leadership of three *literati* civilians, and another who is a military man, so the Chinese priest has hired a large house for a chapel. Our old Ouang at Ea-Ky continues his miracles by means of holy water. He drives away devils, cures the sick, and even the pagans apply to him, which explains the great number of conversions. But a chapel is sadly wanted, as we still have the old granary in which to say Mass, where you forbade women coming, as gambling and opium smoking went on in the room underneath. It is impossible to hear confessions there. In many other stations Catechumens are increasing, and we are simply overwhelmed."

In another letter we are reminded that three poor missionaries cannot superintend properly so many stations full of converts, extending over four prefectures, where there are at least 800,000 infidels, and the missionaries are like drops of water in the ocean. It is not the insufficiency of our labours, but of our priests that is to be deplored. Without any exaggeration, a hundred missionaries could find plenty of serious labour, and in ten years they would not be sufficient, as fresh districts would be opened on all sides. Our Christians, therefore, would be far more numerous were it not that the missionaries are no longer able to cope with their work among such multitudes of Catechumens.

XI.
OUR WORKERS AND THEIR WANTS.

IN the preceding pages I have given, at some length, my views of the Chinese, and also, as far as my limits will permit, I have in a general way described the present state of the mission, and the grounds which we see for hoping for better results in the future than have been achieved in the past. In the following section it is proposed to describe in somewhat greater detail our resources and the methods of our work. The illustrations in this little book represent some of our work, and I will here describe those which are not depicted in the photographs, as well as those that are. As each one of our several works entails expense, it is hardly necessary to point out to the reader that in describing our various works, I am at the same time indicating the various needs of the mission.

The Missionaries.—In the desperate contest between heaven and hell for the souls of men, priests are the proper officials deputed to fight for God and His Catholic Church, and to win from the demon slaves who without their intervention would be lost for ever. Peaceable

OUR WORKERS AND THEIR WANTS. 89

soldiers of the cross they effect immense conquests for the true faith ; indefatigable labourers they sow the good seed of salvation in all directions, often fertilizing it by their sufferings, and sometimes by their blood. They are the main springs of every work undertaken for the conversion of the heathens who are perishing in thousands. Therefore, the need of missionaries is most urgent among these poor pagans, so that these souls wandering in darkness may have a chance of receiving a ray of hope.

The Seminaries.—In obedience to the Holy See, and to supply the paucity of priests, everything is being done to train native priests who are indispensable on the mission. In the " Petit Séminaire " at Chusan, there are forty youths, studying Latin and other sciences under a French missionary, so as later to become learned clergymen with attainments superior to those of the Chinese *literati*. In the "Grand Séminaire" the students apply themselves to theology, which is taught in Latin and in one European language, and they also follow other classes to acquire knowledge that will be useful in their future ministry. It is really important that the native clergy should be highly educated in a country where learning, though based on the teachings of Confucius, and of the most antiquated description, is held in such great esteem by all ranks of people, from the highest to the lowest. Every Chinese boy constantly hears the proverb that " ministers and generals are not born in office," and that the only way to rise in life is by the pursuit of learning and the severe competitive examinations, the principle of which has been adopted nowadays in Europe. In every city of China there is the examination hall with small cells for students, and larger apartments for the examiners, and places where men are stationed to watch that the students have no assistance in their labours.[1] There have been instances when a grandfather of eighty, his son and grandson, have competed in the same examination for the same degree, which in one case was won by the old man. At Foo-chow, in 1889, nine candidates aged eighty, and two aged ninety, went through some examinations with much credit, and men of sixty, if they do not succeed in gaining any of the three higher degrees, receive an honorary one in recompense of their industry.[2]

"In the province of Anhui," says Mr. Smith, "thirty-five of the competitors were over eighty years of age, and eighteen over ninety! Could any other country afford a spectacle like this?"

Brothers,—These have a double vocation. They instruct our orphan boys in different trades for their livelihood, and educate these poor children as good Christians. Of the boys entrusted to their care, some are taught

---

[1] *A Cycle of Cathay,* chap. ii   W. A. P. Martin.
[2] *Chinese Characteristics,* chap. iv.   Rev. A. Smith.

agriculture on a farm belonging to the mission,[1] others become tailors, shoemakers, carpenters, &c., and it is also desirable that they should be taught the weaving of satin, which would be a very lucrative employment. Had they a good European artisan, there would be plenty of work on account of the great quantity of the satin required for embroideries; therefore, during his visit to France, Monseigneur Reynaud intends to seek for some lay brothers acquainted with the process of weaving.

The Brothers are also in demand as teachers in respectable pagan families, who desire their sons to be instructed in some European languages and sciences, and this naturally brings the best families in contact with the Catholic missionaries.

Sisters of Charity of St. Vincent de Paul.—Their work has been frequently mentioned in these pages, and it will not be necessary to say much about them here. Besides, they direct many of the good works which I have still to mention. These include no less than 8 hospitals, 4 hospices, 5 dispensaries, 10 schools, and 5 orphanages—the sisters being in

---

[1] Respecting the acquisition of land and houses in China, a right secured to the missionaries after the "Arrow War," by the French, it may be well to mention that very often in the interior the local officials will oppose the purchase as much as they can, and we are told by Mr. Martin that "a favourite mode of nipping new missions in the bud has been for the local officials to refuse consent, and apply the bamboo to all persons concerned in a sale. Hereafter such proceedings will not be so frequent, but no one who knows China imagines that they will cease."—*A Cycle of Cathay*, chap. xv., p. 443. W. A. P. Martin.

number 35, including, as I have stated, several natives. I will only add to this statement, that their influence among all classes in the Vicariate is very great, and that we could hardly wish for a more eloquent argument for the religion which we represent than the one which is furnished by their presence, and the work which is accomplished by their devotion.

Virgins of Purgatory.—The religious of this Institute are exclusively composed of natives. Their work, like that of the Sisters of Charity, consists to a great extent in the management of orphanages, schools, and institutions for women. Their special devotion, as is shown by their official title, is to the Holy Souls, and often to the most abandoned among them. Each day they offer for the solace of these poor souls, their works, their sufferings, and all their satisfactions. The foundation is a recent one, made in response to the expressed wishes of the Holy See ; their vows are the usual ones of religion, but they are made annually. The Community consists mostly of young women, and they give us the greatest hopes for the future, as well as the deepest consolation at the present time.

Catechists.—Like sentinels on outpost duty, these men prepare the way for the missionaries, by instructing Catechumens, settling local difficulties, preaching to the pagans, baptizing the dying, and leading the devotions on Sundays, where there is no priest to say Mass, in the chapels of which the Catechists are in charge. They

COMMUNITY OF THE VIRGINS OF PURGATORY.
(The Cross marks those who have taken Vows.)

are chosen among youthful and intelligent Christians who have no vocation for the ecclesiastical state, and for three or four years they learn their duties in a preparatory school, after which they acquire practical experience by going out with the missionaries. When they are married, they are sent to places where their services are most needed. A regular battalion of these Catechists is required, and Monseigneur Reynaud often cherishes the dream of "A Society of the Seventy-two Disciples," so as to be able to send one to each of the seventy-two Prefectures of Tché-Kiang.

Schools.—This is one of the most vital works of the mission, in which the Christianizing of children is concerned. They must be instructed very young, and taken away as much as possible from pagan surroundings. To do this properly, the schools should be near the missionaries. There are central schools in all the chief mission stations, where the children are completely separated from bad influences, and are taught to practise their religion by their teachers and by the good example they see around them, whereas children who have not had this advantage are recognisable at a glance, as they do not comprehend their religion at all well.

Another very important consideration is the following with regard to schools. They are often found to be most useful as a means of furthering conversions, as, according to a French missionary, "When the infant comes to school, his father will soon follow the child to the church," and these dear children, like St. John Baptist, fill the valleys and bring low the mountains and hills, by opening to their parents the path leading to our Blessed Saviour.[1]

Catechumens.—The same remarks about the children may be applied to the Catechumens, who, unless they can spend a few months in our residences, near the priests and the church, never become really reliable Christians. The example and the daily instruction of the missionaries, the absence from pagan surroundings, and family cares, mean everything to them, as it is chiefly by means of sight and hearing they can be thoroughly christianized. An association to further the religious instruction of poor Catechumens on the Catholic missions already exists in France at the Carmelites of Tours, and is zealously supported by pious ladies. The Catechumens who cannot spend a short time in the mission station may know their catechism, but they do not understand their religion so perfectly as the others.

Hospitals.—The following lines, written 27th February, 1897, by one of the community of the Sisters of Charity at Ning-Po, will point out the good effected by a Catholic hospital :—

"The heathens come to this hospital with the same

---

[1] Taken from the *Lettres de Jersey*, vol. xiii., p. 13. The Editor of this publication kindly lent some volumes to the translator. The articles in them deal with the Jesuit vicariate of Kiang-nan, which is a near neighbour of Tché-Kiang.

confidence as ever. Two pagan women, sisters unhappily married to opium smokers, came here to ask for baptism, as a passport to heaven. The eldest, who was here last year had been at home since her cure, where she has been telling all she knows of religion learned from us, to her young consumptive sister, who came here to die after being baptized. Some days later we heard that the eldest sister was ill again, and so serious was her state that we were obliged to gratify her wish for baptism. When slightly better she came here to prepare for her death to which she was quite resigned. The two little daughters-in-law of these sisters have also departed this life about the same time, and, favoured by the grace of conversion, one of them was afraid of going to heaven, for fear she should find her mother-in-law there, but we succeeded in convincing her that in heaven her mother-in-law could never ill-treat her again." [1]

More than three thousand patients pass annually through the hospitals. Most of them go away cured,

---

[1] It is very usual to see in Chinese houses a little girl, the drudge of the women, who is cruelly beaten on all occasions. This is the future daughter-in-law often purchased for a dollar out of a heathen orphanage. Should the child break down, she is callously thrown out to die, and she is fortunate if she happen to be picked up by a Sister of Charity, or some humane person, and conveyed to the hospital. But if the girl grows up well in spite of the inhuman usage, she is married to the son for whom she has been purchased, and instantly is treated with consideration in the household, and in due time her own turn arrives to have a daughter-in-law to maltreat precisely in the same manner.

and tell their relations and friends how well they have been treated. This favourable report lessens prejudices against the foreigners; increases esteem for the sisters, spreads the knowledge of religion, and induces other sick people to come to the hospital, where they are often converted, or return later to be baptized and to die there. Cases of patients wilfully choosing to die in paganism are almost unknown, and, as a rule, they all become Christians in their last moments, and the baptisms *in articulo mortis* at the hour of death, amount to three hundred yearly. There are also dispensaries attached to the hospitals frequented annually by 100,000 people, while the visits paid by the sisters to the sick in their own homes are over 35,000 in the year.

Asylums.—These are for destitute old men, whose spiritual and corporal necessities are worthy of compassion. Inured to suffering, they give little trouble, never complain, and are grateful for the interest taken in them. It is really a pleasure to see how they obey, and even forestall the least wish of the sister, trying to help her as far as they can. They are attentive to the religious instruction of the missionary, and are eager for baptism. This charitable work makes a good impression upon pagan Chinese, old age being held in great veneration by these people, who think a great deal more of kindness to the aged than to the children.

Orphanages.—Were the missionaries to adopt every child that is abandoned, especially in time of scarcity, they would be overwhelmed and their resources quickly exhausted. It is a great trial to be forced to reject so many, and Monseigneur Reynaud has often been aroused at night by the cries of infants left secretly at his door, to whom he could give nothing but the sacrament of baptism. Those fortunate children who are taken into the orphanages receive the most devoted care, and are brought up as simple and laborious Christians, who are settled in the world as advantageously as possible. Some are placed in Christian families, while others form Christian villages which are like an oasis in the desert of paganism. Among the orphans cripples have a privileged place, as they require more care. The lame, paralytic, blind, deaf mutes, those suffering from spinal and other dreadful deformities, as well as idiots, are all in this category, and have to be maintained all their lives.

Home for Widows.—There is a refuge for these women at Ning-Po which ought to be enlarged, and others established in other parts of the province.

Workers in Embroidery.—This new but little-known enterprise, the organization of which has occupied two years, is an excellent means of helping poor Christian and pagan families. Assisted by charitable people there is now a workroom with eighty women, and work is given out to fifty families by the Sisters of Charity, who have the management and the merit of this industry. It is a nice honest employment, and a great relief to poor people, while the wages gained by the wives strengthen the affection of the husbands, and bring peace and means to the household. Then the pagan women in communication with the Sisters see and learn much that is good from them, and sincere conversions are frequent. To ensure the success of this industry many openings are required for the sale of the work.

Churches and Chapels.—This subject has been left to the last, though it be not the least important. People are always more ready to assist the poor than to contribute to the erection of churches, although in Ireland this is less the case than in other countries, the pence of the poor Irish being generally the foundation of many noble churches.

Now, chapels and churches are necessary in a mission for the celebration of Holy Mass, the administration of the Sacraments, and the observance of Sunday. In Tché-Kiang, covered with magnificent heathen pagodas, the want of suitable chapels is more felt by the converts, who are humbled at seeing how few are our " Kong So " to those of the idols.

This account of our work, writes Monseigneur Reynaud, is also a list of our wants, and in order that they should be better understood, a few figures are added to show the extent of some of our expenses.

	£	s.	d.
The annual keep of a Priest	20	0	0
Religious (Brother, or Sister of Charity)	16	0	0
Seminarist	9	0	0
Virgin of Purgatory	10	5	0
Catechist	7	5	0
Patient (in hospital)	3	5	0
Aged man (in hospice)	2	10	0
Orphan or Catechumen	2	0	0
Widows, school-children, and infants (each)	1	12	0

There is just one thing that is not inscribed upon the list of good works, in Chinese Catholic missions, an achievement that God alone can fully appreciate, viz., the physical and mental wear and tear of the missionary, who, sometimes exposed to a sudden martyrdom, more frequently dies by slow inches from the effects of privations and overwork. Although he never complains, but joyfully sacrifices his life in the service of God, he asks, nevertheless, two things from his brethren in Europe: alms and prayers. As long as he lives, he will continue this supplication, for by prayers and alms he can obtain the dearest wish of a missionary heart—the salvation of souls. The merit arising from this double gift is the most precious treasure, the sweetest joy, and the best recompense he can desire for his benefactors.

L. of C.

XII.
PARTING WORDS.

SOME of our readers may think, after perusing these pages, that I am myself a little bit too much of a Chinaman. Whether this be a matter for praise or reproach, I do not deny that I really love China as my adopted country where I hope to live and die. I found China far more beautiful and better in general than I had ever expected, and, in the midst of so many ill-conditioned pagans, I have met with such numbers of simple and honest souls, that my trials and disappointments have been alleviated by much consolation. Few missionaries will contradict this assertion, as China is a land of exile which they love, and which they rarely leave without regret. When obliged by ill-health or other reasons to depart, it is always on the understanding that they will be allowed to return there. They positively yearn for China, and are only happy on seeing its shores again. To those, however, who have not been so fortunate on the mission, I should say that they must have had the mishap of meeting with a bad set of people, and that in other better disposed localities their labours would certainly have been more successful. To those who persist in asking why there are still so few neophytes notwithstanding our efforts, we must always answer that these exertions would have been far more successful, in spite of violent persecutions, were it not for the paucity of missionaries, who, although they have certainly increased within the last fifty years, are even now in the proportion of one to four hundred thousand infidels. To appreciate the relative progress of religion we should bear in mind that the pagan Chinese, which according to some historians are over 400,000,000,[1] far exceed the Catholics throughout the whole world; consequently, when we reflect on the number of the missionaries and the sum total of annual conversions, we need not be discouraged.

What is really most required in China for the spread of the faith is missionaries. Were there more priests we should have more Catechumens, as one missionary can only attend to a certain number of converts, who have to be tested, instructed, and trained in the ways of Christian life, all of which entail much labour, and often many journeys. He must have as many catechism classes as there are localities where Catechumens reside; then he must settle various difficulties that always arise among the converts, such as family persecution, and worries of all kinds, while the Mandarins are always ready to complicate the simplest cases; so that a

---

[1] See, however, p 19.

missionary may be kept stationary for a long time by one piece of business.

We are also in great need of pecuniary assistance. Just as soldiers must have arms, the missionaries must have funds, to build the chapel, the school, and the little presbytery, which are as it were the outposts of the mission; to say nothing of the schoolmaster, the cook, a servant, and a band of young converts studying Christian doctrine. Our strongholds are represented by our great churches, central schools, orphanages, hospitals, dispensaries, asylums and various other works of charity. Thus, there are many ways of exhausting the missionary's purse, though he may himself live on very little, as our converts will never let him die of starvation, but are always ready to share their houses and food with him. Still a large family of orphans and destitute people frequently depend on him for their support. Hence if we do not choose to assist the missions by sending out numerous priests and sufficient material aid, it will be useless to talk of China as a land of the future for the Catholic Church.

Moreover, to do something for China would appear to be a special duty for Great Britain; but whereas France, Italy, Spain, Belgium, and Holland have many representatives there doing good work for the people, there is at present only one English-speaking priest[1] in

---

[1] This is the Rev. John M'Veigh, C.M., of Pekin, who has been recently making a tour in Great Britain and Ireland. We are

the whole Empire. This is the more to be regretted, as
British sailors, merchants, and traders in the Chinese
ports far outnumber those of other European countries.
Certainly it is but just to acknowledge that in the
matter of Protestant missions, England shows plenty
of generosity with regard to the conversion of China.
Every year she sends out bands of missionaries with
handsome stipends, often at the same time that hundreds
of cases of that poison called opium are introduced as
British merchandise. Ought not Catholic England and
Ireland try to do something to repair the errors of
Protestant and commercial England? This would be
only to pay a debt and to expiate a wrong. The means
are simple enough; send us money if you can, but
above all send us men. As regards the former, I do
not ask for large sums. Are there any so poor who
cannot afford even a penny? Yet it is precisely these
pence that do wonders. They support the apostles who
convert the heathens; they build churches and chapels
in a land where pagodas abound; they contribute to
the education of priests in the seminaries; they maintain
the old, the sick, and the orphans, all so numerous
among us: and without the help of these pence how
many heathens are there who would die hopeless after a
life full of privation.

---

indebted to him for much information about China, which has been
of great use in preparing this edition of Monseigneur Reynaud's
notes.—(EDITOR.)

With regard to missionaries themselves, they should be men of physical strength and real self-sacrifice, and should be properly trained for the peculiar hardships of this mission. It is the great desire of Monseigneur Reynaud's heart to have some English, or English-speaking missionaries. For one thing, their influence, in counteracting the peculiar obstacles raised by the Protestant missions, would be very valuable. On this subject, an English lady at Ning-Po, writes : " I hope that the presence of English-speaking priests would prevent our Protestant compatriots from behaving in the very objectionable way they often do—not at Ning-Po, where we have the *élite*, many of them educated gentlemen, but in the interior, where with some of them their one creed seems to be preaching against Catholicity." It is hardly necessary to point out that all this could be far more easily dealt with by those who speak the same language as these 'objectionable' ministers, and who from proximity to them at home, are acquainted with their doctrines and their methods. Besides, it is wrong to leave the Chinese under the belief that the English people are universally members of what they call the English Religion.[1] To further this aim of Monseigneur Reynaud, a fund for

---

[1] The presence of Sir Nicholas O'Connor, as British Ambassador, for some years at Pekin, that most successful of diplomatists and most fervent of Irish Catholics, did something towards breaking down this idea among the Mandarins and the court officials; but his influence did not so directly reach the masses.

PARTING WORDS.

China has been started in connection with the Irish branch of the Arch-Confraternity of St. Joseph, Protector of the souls of Purgatory. It is the work of the Confraternity to provide priests for foreign missions who will belong to St. Joseph and to the Holy Souls. No more glorious work could be looked forward to by the Apostolic student than to devote himself to this immense Empire with its millions of pagan souls, so many of whom show themselves willing to see the light of the true faith when it is brought before their eyes. It is hoped that many will offer themselves before long, and the fund to which we refer has been started for the special support and assistance of such students.[1]

Another important assistance is prayer for the success of our undertaking; and who is there who cannot pray for the conversion of souls, and their perseverance in the faith? Many conversions may be attributed less to the labours of the missionary than to the fervent prayers of many an obscure person living far away. In their retired cloisters, monks and nuns may in this way give great help by their prayers to the evangelization of China. Thus by alms and by prayers everyone can become a missionary, closing the gates of hell, and opening those

---

[1] Any contributions to the China Fund for St. Joseph's Young Priests, will be acknowledged in *St. Joseph's Sheaf*, which is the quarterly organ of the Arch-Confraternity of St. Joseph. The address of the Secretary is 7, Eblana-Terrace, Kingstown, who will also forward full particulars as to the Fund, and the Masses offered for those who contribute to it.

of heaven to innumerable heathens. Self-interes brings to China people in search of the wealth it contains. Shall we be less eager where far superior interests are concerned, and should we not endeavour to do all in our power to cultivate this fertile soil giving us such hopes for the advancement of religion?

Therefore, may this immense Empire be invaded by numerous fervent and apostolic men planting the cross in every direction, and saving souls from the mire of paganism. In the knowledge of the true faith may those generous and upright beings, who, led away by error, are yet sighing for happiness, soon find among us that which they desire.

Da Mihi Animas!

www.ingramcontent.com/pod-product-compliance
Lightning Source LLC
Chambersburg PA
CBHW030903170426
43193CB00009BA/720